52 JOHN DEERE Backyard Landscaping Projects

Designing, Planting, and Building the Yard of Your Dreams ONE WEEKEND at a Time

Creative Publishing international

CHANHASSEN, MINNESOTA
www.creativepub.com

© 2007

Creative Publishing international, Inc.

18705 Lake Drive East

Chanhassen, Minnesota 55317

800-328-3895

www.creativepub.com

All rights reserved.

President/CEO: Ken Fund

Technical Editor: Karen Ruth

Editor and Project Manager: Betsy Gammons

Creative Director: Rosalind Loeb Wanke

Art Director: David Martinell

Production Manager: Barbara States

Design: John Hall Design Group   www.johnhalldesign.com

All illustrations by Chuck Lockhart with the exception of Lorraine Dey, page 22; Mario Ferro, page 40.

Jacket front: Courtesy of ICI Paints/www.icipaints.com, bottom, (right);

Clive Nichols/www.clivenichols.co.uk, top, (middle & right); bottom, (left & second from left);

Jessie Walker/www.jessiewalker.com, middle; middle, (right)

Jacket back: Dency Kane/www.dencykane.com, middle, (right); top, (left); Clive Nichols/www.clivenichols.co.uk, middle (left);

Allan Penn, bottom (left); top (right); Courtesy of Thomas Sanderson Ltd./www.thomas-sanderson.co.uk, bottom (right);

Jessie Walker/www.jessiewalker.com, top (second from left); middle

ISBN-13: 978-1-58923-363-8

ISBN-10: 1-58923-363-8

10 9 8 7 6 5 4 3 2 1

Library of Congress Cataloging-in-Publication Data

Hampshire, Kristen.

  John Deere 52 backyard landscaping projects : designing, planting, and building the yard of your dreams one weekend at a time / Kristen Hampshire.

    p. cm.

  Includes index.

  ISBN 1-58923-363-8

  1. Landscape gardening. 2. Garden structures--Design and construction. 3. Garden ornaments and furniture--Design and construction. I. Deere & Company. II. Title. III. Title: John Deere fifty-two backyard landscaping projects.

  SB473.H33 2007

  635.9--dc22

2007021451

CIP

Printed in Singapore

Contents

PART ONE

Dream It, Design It, Do It Yourself

When you look out your window, what do you see? What do you envision? These are two entirely different questions, as you consider what elements your landscape provides. Whether plant beds or playgrounds, which features will transform your space into a better place to relax, entertain, or play? If you can dream it, you can design it. Build a better backyard patio for dining, plant a chef's garden with all the right ingredients, and create a nook in your landscape where you can enjoy the rewards of your hard work. All this is possible—you just need the right plan.

Start with a Plan

As conscientious homeowners, we're in hot pursuit of curb appeal. Achieving an admirable landscape is a passion for some, and the art and science of lawn care and crafting an outdoor room has evolved into a robust industry. Bombarding us with inspiration are books and magazines, television programs geared toward do-it-yourselfers, and a bounty of products designed to turn the great outdoors into an extension of the home.

Possibilities are endless—like choosing from a menu that culminates the best dishes from every restaurant in the world. You feel full just looking at the options. Meanwhile, the more ideas we gather from these resources, the more potential landscape projects we file into our mental to-do lists. Where should you start?

Whether you just moved into a new home, or you're quite settled and want to improve the space you're in, spend some time dreaming and seriously considering what activities you enjoy outdoors. One homeowner's backyard might serve as an informal sports arena, while another uses the space as a quiet refuge. Someone with a large family that hosts barbecue gatherings will go to the drawing board with different expectations than a townhouse-dweller who just acquired their first, compact plot of land. Use of space will dictate how you plan your design.

Also, evaluate how much time you are willing to spend maintaining the space. A busy professional, who wants to treat the patio like a vacation spot, may not have time for careful gardening. Or, that same time-crunched homeowner may love nothing more than pruning and cutting—methodical lawn care practices are good medicine for some. Be realistic about your capabilities. How do you want to spend your time outdoors? Rest assured, there are professionals to help you manage maintenance or take on larger projects if your lofty plans exceed your capabilities. (See Going Pro on page 21.) But you can take on the projects in this book by yourself. If you do, you'll gain the satisfaction of creating something from scratch.

YOUR PROPERTY IS AN EXPRESSION of your personality, and you can design a landscape that serves as a retreat or a playground.

What's Your Pleasure?

Because your landscape represents your personality, each element is an expression of your favorite colors, hobbies, and style preferences. Begin defining a plan by asking yourself some questions. This is a preliminary exercise that will guide you as you set goals for your ultimate plan. Once you figure out which features are most important, you can begin to choose projects that fulfill these priorities.

Your Lifestyle

- What activities do you enjoy outdoors?
- Are your outdoor pursuits active (sports, swimming, gardening) or meditative (reading, dining, napping in a hammock)?
- When do you spend most of your time outdoors—in the daytime or evening? Are there areas of your property you wish were better lit?
- What time of year do you enjoy your yard—mostly in warm weather, or year-round? Do you want a space that protects you from the elements, or do you generally avoid the outdoors in undesirable weather?
- Do you entertain often? If so, how many people do you generally host, and are gatherings casual, active, or geared around outdoor dining?
- Do you have children? Do they use your yard for play?
- Do you have pets?
- What inspires you to improve your landscape?

WITH THE ARRAY of design elements in this landscape, from stepping stones to ground cover and carefully pruned shrubbery, you can easily accomplish the project in phases.

Your Design

- Which phrase best describes your attitude? Free and easy; prim and proper; detail oriented; or bigger is better.
- Do you prefer straight or curved lines?
- What do you find more appealing, a manicured topiary or flowing ornamental grasses?
- What are your favorite colors?
- Do you prefer uniformity (a palette of several distinctive plants), or are you eclectic (the more varieties, the merrier)?
- Which of these elements most appeals to your senses? Water, fire, stone, or wood.
- What are your goals for gardening? Growing vegetables, herbs, or cut flowers.
- What is your favorite existing feature in the backyard? Is there a specific tree, a patio area, or a spot you find aesthetically pleasing?

Your Property

- Are there utilities or eyesores you wish to hide?
- Is your yard private or exposed?
- Are there permanent structures or plantings you must work around, such as a large evergreen tree or concrete patio that you don't want to remove?
- Does your property sit on a slope, have areas with poor drainage, or contain other topographical quirks (ruts, sunken areas, etc)?
- Is your yard shady, exposed to full sunlight, or a combination of the two?
- What existing plants or features do you love?
- What features are priorities for removal?
- Do you plan to maintain your yard yourself (mowing, pruning), or do you expect to hire a professional?

Some of these questions were probably easier to answer than others. All of them shed light on your wants and needs in a landscape. For example, have you ever really thought about preferring topiary over ornamental grasses, or whether you truly find curved bed lines attractive? While considering possibilities, don't forget to get feedback from others who use the space. If your design must accommodate more than one person—say, your children, spouse, or a housemate—then you should call an informal meeting and collect their insights. (Of course, if your six-year-old insists that a jungle gym bigger than the house is a top priority, you can safely scale down this project.)

Your Wish List

By now, you can set some short- and long-term goals for your landscape. For example, immediately, you want to create an herb garden and enjoy your landscape at night. Long term, you hope to grow a variety of vegetables, you want to create a private, outdoor space where you can escape to read a book, and you envision separate areas in your backyard dedicated to entertaining, play, and gardening.

Based on these ideas, and note that they start simple, you can start by planting a container garden with herbs. Install low-voltage landscape lighting, which will enhance your night views. Down the road, you can work on building a pond, a play area, and a patio with an outdoor kitchen. You might incorporate stepping stones that lead to these areas, and install groundcover in places you're tired of mowing, and low growing plants in these areas to differentiate them. See how plans unfold?

Before you head to the drawing board, write down several main goals for your property. While creating a plan and choosing projects, always refer to this list. It will remind you that the smaller-scale tasks add up to a big-impact back yard ... over time. Most of all, prioritizing your goals based on your lifestyle, design preferences, and realistic maintenance expectations, will assure that your ultimate project truly suits your needs.

Imagine Your Space

Before putting pen to paper to establish a physical design for your landscape, reserve the time to brainstorm. If your goal is to create an outdoor room, and your priority is to start with a concrete slab, have you thought about all the ways you can convert this surface into a more aesthetic platform? For example, you can stain concrete. Or, you can use it as a foundation and lay bluestone on it, grouting together seams for a tile effect. What about covering the slab entirely with stained, wood planks? Don't let all the choices overwhelm you. Based on the questions you answered earlier, use your style to direct decisions on materials. Then, do your homework and dream. This is the fun part about landscape design!

Where do you find inspiration? Here are some resources where you'll find great ideas:

Books: Don't limit yourself to books that only cover horticulture or gardening. Leaf through titles on interior design, construction, even travel. You can capture elements from the concepts you see in these books and translate them to the outdoors. For example, if you discover a fantastic rug in an interior magazine, why not find a way to incorporate a rug on your patio? There are weatherproof rugs you can buy in stores, and if the patio is sheltered, you might choose a floor covering from an antique shop to infuse a bit of shabby-chic in your outdoor dining room. While reading a travel book, you may decide to convert your deck into a Mediterranean-

QUICK TIP

Dig safe. Remember to check for buried cables before you dig. Most communities have a free service you can call that will mark your property for any concealed electrical, cable, gas, phone, and all other lines. Not sure how to locate this service? Call your utility company and ask for a recommendation.

inspired retreat. Or perhaps a construction book will provoke thought. Keep an open mind.

Magazines: Garden and design magazines are plentiful with the growing popularity of landscaping. The newsstand is teeming with ideas to improve your space.

Television: We're an HGTV generation, and if we're not actually doing a project ourselves, we can watch someone else do the work and learn from their experience. Tune in and see what ideas you can pull from these programs. Professionals on do-it-yourself segments generally provide step-by-step directions.

Vacation: What did you like best about your beach vacation? Was it the poolside cabana or the sound of splashing water? Did the rustling of natural grasses on dunes lull you into a meditative state? You can mimic these sensory pleasers. Ponds, a collection of ornamental grasses, or a pergola—these are projects you can manage that will re-create vacation ambiance on your humble plot of land.

Neighbors: A simple tour of your neighborhood will spark ideas for plantings, patios, play areas, you name it. Whatever the project, it has probably been done. So next time you're invited to a friend's barbecue, take a closer look at the property's outdoor elements. What appeals to you? You don't have to worry about copying a concept, because there are so many variations on a theme that yours will certainly look different.

Retailers: Shop around local nurseries, homes centers, and mass merchandisers that sell everything from plants to plywood. New products on the market make completing outdoor projects easier than ever. For example, you can purchase kits for drip irrigation (see page 48) or outdoor lighting (see page 184). And professionals can provide valuable information. Ask questions.

Measure and Map Out Elements

Your property is a living canvas. While you are the designated artist, and the colors, textures, and mood you infuse are yours to choose, you still must stay within the lines. There are limits: mostly the size of your space, but also topographical quirks that you must account for during the project planning process. Generally speaking, you can work around features with a little creative thinking. You probably won't remove a century-old oak tree to install your deck; but you can always construct a half-moon shape or even create a peep hole, of sorts, so the tree appears to grow from the middle of the deck. Before delving into any project, you should sketch a detailed map of your property, drawing in existing plants, beds, trees, and structures.

Capture a Close-Up

Walk your property, and survey the entire space—front, back, and side yard—with a critical eye. Of course, you will see the obvious: plant beds, large trees, and a supersized grill. However, observation beyond these elements will uncover information that is important to consider as you install landscape and other structures. For example, do you notice that puddles tend to collect in the center of your back lawn? You'll want to know this before creating a path that leads right into a potential mud bath. Also, what about that clunky air conditioning unit in the side yard? Or the neighbor's unsightly neon-yellow swing set? Certainly, you can block these eyesores if you choose. The key is to notice what you *want* to see, and what you'd like to hide. This is part of your job during the close-up tour of your property.

Following are other characteristics you'll want to note while you survey your property. Make a list of these items as you take your tour. That way, you can refer to your inventory and translate them into rough sketch. This drawing will help you decide which projects to tackle first.

Plantings

Take note of all existing plantings: gardens, flower beds, bushes, trees, and ground cover. While you're playing plant inspector, look for thriving plants and weaklings that struggle, despite your efforts. There is no better time to amend soil and renovate a lawn than while you're digging into a planting or other landscape project. So make a list of the plants and trees you have, and whether they look healthy.

Water and Electricity

Water spigots and outdoor electrical outlets are essential for certain landscape projects, such as drip irrigation and low-voltage lighting. Note the location of these utilities. Also, if you already have landscape lighting, mark the locations of each fixture. The same goes for in-ground irrigation systems. You want to avoid disrupting wiring for these systems, unless you plan to replace them. Be sure to include electrical and cable boxes in your survey. If you already know the location of underground wiring, you'll also want to make note of that in your sketch.

Structures

Think hardscape: decks, sheds, playground equipment—anything not living is a structure you must build around or demolish to replace. Hardscape refers to pavers, stonework, or retaining walls. Also, don't forget to figure in places where you temporarily set up a structure. For example, if you have a portable swinging chair that you like to set under a shade tree in your yard, be sure to write this down. You may want to incorporate a permanent seating space in your plan, or at least save room for this special furniture.

In the front yard, consider lampposts, benches, walkways, your driveway, and even your front porch. In side yards, pencil in garbage cans, if that's their permanent home. Don't forget to take account for trellises, pergolas, or other frames.

Turf Traits

Turf color and wet spots provide helpful clues about your property's grade. As you walk across your grass, feel for mushy areas where water tends to collect. Notice slopes, ruts, and rough terrain. Are there brown spots? This can indicate poor soil quality, water run-off (to lower spots), or severe sun exposure. You can always choose to do something else with that space besides grow grass, so keep that in mind.

You can obtain a survey, also called a plot plan, from your city or town hall. Double check your site plan against this document to detect any discrepancies.

Sun Spots

Which areas of your yard are sunny and which are shady? Do plant beds get full sun? Do they receive a balanced mix of sun and shade, depending on the time of day? How do trees affect the sunlight on your property? The generous canopy of an oak tree may block light from reaching a nearby plant bed.

Understanding nature's lighting on your property is critical when choosing plants and deciding where to place structures. For example, if your patio is positioned in full sun, you may decide to build a pergola and grow clematis as a living curtain to make the space more comfortable for sitting. As for plant selection, knowing a space's sunlight exposure will ensure that you select tolerant varieties.

Eyesores

Now is when you can make a gripe list—go ahead, vent! That ugly cable box, a gnarly shed, and a neighbor's shabby clothesline always full of—well, you'd rather not know. You can design landscape elements that showcase nature's beauty, or block humans' tasteless contributions to the great outdoors. We've dedicated a whole project section to "shutters," or features that hide undesirables. Pinpoint the eyesores, and choose a project to cover up the unsightly.

ROUND CIRCLES represent trees and ornamentals in this bubble diagram.

Get It On Paper

Convert your list of plants and landscape features onto a rough sketch of your property. A visual representation of your space will help you map out which areas you want to enhance. Once you get it all on paper, you can scratch out plant beds and add new, curvier ones—maybe an island in the middle of your yard, where grass tends to die out. You can draft a patio addition. Remember, if you can dream it, you can design it. But first, you'll want to start with a map of what already exists.

Ideally, you should draw your diagram to scale. To do this properly, you must measure your property, your home, plant beds, and every structure. Scale drawings are helpful because they allow you to make precise decisions about exactly how large your deck should be, how many plants per square foot you must purchase, and so on. Landscape architects prepare scale drawings of their clients' properties, filling in dimensional drawings to bring a plan to life. But you can take a more elementary approach and still create an effective land map that will help you choose and prioritize landscape projects. These less-scientific drawings are called bubble diagrams. They are working outlines that, essentially, convert that list of features you compiled into shapes on a page. A bubble diagram is also a precursor to the scale drawing.

A simple outline of the home serves as the focal point of the bubble diagram. After all, your house is the largest obstacle, in a sense. Circles represent bushes, plantings, and trees. Label abstract boxes, triangles, and circles, which represent various features. The resulting map probably looks more like a kindergarten art project than a plan of your property. But remember—imagination! By blocking out space, you can see what areas need work. You can plot areas for a pond, a display of container plantings, or pencil in where landscape lighting would allow you to make better use of your favorite outdoor areas.

Why not make several photocopies of this bubble diagram? As you mark pages in this book with projects you want to try, you can pencil in the design. As your plan evolves, you'll probably need to remove elements before you can add new ones. Replace ground cover with hardscape, or vice-versa. Install a pond rather than a playground. (Probably not the children's choice, but who's performing the hard labor?!) Referring to the project priority list you created earlier, you can begin to think in phases. By breaking down your wish list into manageable chunks, or weekend projects, you can gradually transform your space.

A SCALE DRAWING of your property is a handy tool for landscape planning. Take the time to measure every element of your space, and get those specifications on paper. That way, you'll rest assured that the projects you choose will truly fit your yard's layout.

A Site Plan

You wouldn't depart on a road trip to a new vacation spot without consulting a map. Though you might eventually arrive at the destination, you could have saved yourself time and energy by planning a route first. Similarly, you can dig plant beds and tear up a portion of your lawn to build a pond. But if you later realize that your bed is two feet away from a sunny area that would have supported the flowers you wanted to plant, you'll end up digging again. You need a site plan.

A site plan is a to-scale drawing. You'll spend some time to ensure the plan is accurate, but understanding exactly where each permanent element (house, driveway, paths, trees) fits on your property will help you determine where, to the inch, you can create new features.

Here is what you'll need to measure your property and create a site plan:

- **Tape measures** (100-foot and 25-foot [30.5 and 7.6-m])
- **Pen**
- **Large sheet of paper**
- **An artist's clipboard**
- **Stakes** (10 to 12)
- **String and a string level** (if you want to measure grade changes for building a retaining wall)

As you dream up ways to enhance existing landscape features, visualize how these elements will fit in your property. Sketch possibilities on tissue overlays, and place them over your site plan. You can use several layers of tissue to represent various project stages. The first tissue might contain foundation plantings and major structures. The second might include a water feature, additional plantings, or a plan for a seasonal planting change-out, and so on.

Create the site plan by recording accurate measurements of your home, property lines, and existing landscape features.

1. Draw a rough sketch: Outline your house on the piece of paper. This will serve as a reference point.

2. Measure your house: Start at a corner of your house, and measure the length with the longer tape measure. Record this measurement. Then measure items like windows, your front door, porches, or other extensions. Such details are important for plant placement. Next, measure the width of your house, again accounting for windows and other elements. Sketch in drain spouts, electrical meters, and cable boxes.

3. Measure your property: First, measure the distance from each corner of your house to property lines (four corners). Mark each spot with a stake; note this distance on your drawing. Finally, measure the lengths of the property lines and distances between corners and stakes along the lines. (By this point, you will have staked the perimeter of your property.)

4. Measure driveways and paths: Measure the distances from property corners to where driveways, fences, or paths cross property lines. Measure the dimensions of these elements. Record dimensions on your sketch.

5. Include trees and plant beds: To measure tree and shrub placement, start by running your longer measuring tape from the corner of your house to the property line. Set down the tape measure. Next, measure from this tape line to your shrub. (The two measuring tapes will form a T.) Record the distance. For example, the tree is 15 feet (4.6 m) from the house and 6 feet (1.8 m) to the right. Knowing these distances will help you accurately place trees, plant beds, and all structures on your site plan.

Now you are ready to create your to-scale site plan. You'll first need to pick up a few supplies from an art store: 20 by 30 inch (50.8 by 76.2 cm) vellum paper, which will allow you to run blueprint photocopies of your design, once complete. You'll also use a three-sided architect's ruler, which will convert your measurements to scale. A T-square and drafting triangles in 30- or 45-degree shapes will help you draw straight lines and angles. Be sure to use pencil when drawing your site map; we all make mistakes, and the ability to erase them will save you paper and frustration.

Before you begin transferring measurements to the page, you must determine your working scale. Do this by dividing the length of your property by the working length of the paper. Use the largest scale possible for the paper. (Draw a 100-foot [30.5-m] -long property line in a 25-inch [63.5 cm] space, leaving a border on your paper for notes.) One inch (2.5 cm) equals 4 feet (1.2 m).

Start by sketching property lines, and then place your house in the appropriate area. (This is when you'll need your eraser.) Redraw the house to scale, using measurements you collected. Repeat for all elements of the house and landscape. Take your time while drawing the map, and go back outside to measure areas again that don't seem to translate properly on the page. Remember, your site plan is a work in progress, so be patient. The result of your hard work is a fine-tuned map that you can play with as you consider project possibilities.

In addition to creating the bird's-eye-view site plan, create an elevation plan as well. An elevation plan is a side view. This is helpful for visualizing the relative heights of the objects and plantings in your yard. For example, you wouldn't want to install tall shrubs in front of a picture window, but without an elevation plan, you might forget that the window is just 3 feet (0.9 m) from the ground.

Creating a Budget

Phase planning is important for any landscape design, and taking on projects in stages is also kinder to your budget. If you think about it, you can spend as little or as much as you want renovating your landscape—consider the options available in materials alone. You can splurge on a grilling area, equipped with a stone fireplace for cooking, a refrigeration unit, and a mosaic tile countertop and bar. Or, you can build a basic deck, buy a quality grill, and skip the rest. Designing a landscape *is* creating an outdoor room; therefore, budgeting outdoor projects is no different than building a home.

Seriously consider how much you can spend on the total project. How much can you set aside for landscaping during one season, for a month, or every week? Refer to your bubble diagram and priority list, and divide your dream design into stages. Certain projects cost much more than others, so you can choose a handful of high-impact, yet affordable enhancements (container plantings), or dedicate your resources to a single, large-scale project that will serve as a foundation for other improvements in the future. For example, lay pavers to create a living space this season. On weekends, take on small projects like building a window box or installing low-voltage lighting. By year's end, your basic patio will have evolved into a serene, natural room.

Budgeting is also critical if you decide to hire a landscape architect to assist with planning or if you bring on a design and installation firm that will handle labor, as well. The architect can design your project in budget-friendly stage. Just warn him or her that you don't plan to bite off the entire redesign at once. Also, you'll want to know in advance how much you can spend on plants and other materials. A professional can steer you toward affordable annuals so you can splurge on perennials, which are long lasting. Or, if you are exploring various materials to use in a patio area, an architect can specify a job with various options so you can compare pricing. Ultimately, you should not make your final materials choices because of price. Remember, landscaping is an investment in your property, and a long-term decision in cases of structural enhancements. Do it right the first time.

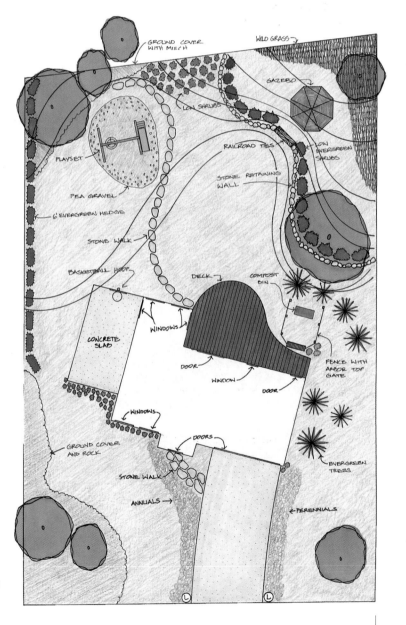

THIS SITE MAP shows the ultimate plan and serves as a reference as you complete the project in phases.

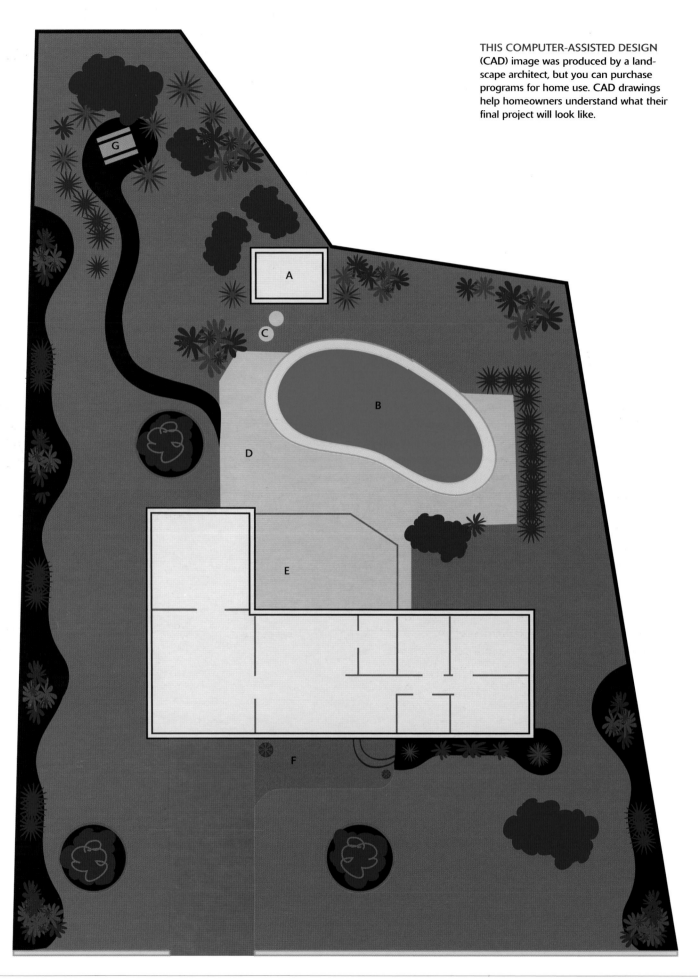

THIS COMPUTER-ASSISTED DESIGN (CAD) image was produced by a landscape architect, but you can purchase programs for home use. CAD drawings help homeowners understand what their final project will look like.

Before hiring a design-installation firm, or any landscape company for that matter, ask these vital questions concerning licensing, certification, and insurance:

- Do you belong to a professional trade association? Which one?

- Are you licensed or certified?

- Do you have proof of insurance and bonding?

- Can you show me examples of your work? (Pictures or actual properties you can drive by to see end results)

- What is your specialty?

Going Pro

Landscape architects are licensed professionals schooled in landscape design. They are the creativity behind building projects, the idea people who can introduce possibilities. Often, landscape architects work within design firms. These companies are one-stop shops, providing design/build and installation services under one roof. This setup is convenient for homeowners who want a seamless transition from planning to execution.

Before and after shots are inspirational, showing us how a bare lawn was transformed into a horticultural oasis or how a concrete slab evolved into an outdoor kitchen. When hiring a landscape architect, the most important first step is to review their portfolio. What jobs were challenging? Which ones capture his or her design personality? Ask the architect to communicate strengths. What type of work does the firm prefer (make sure it's residential), and does the company have installation capabilities?

Landscape architects work with clients to develop the type of phase plans we discussed. They come to the table with ideas, and are an excellent resource. You may not feel comfortable taking on a large-scale, structural project without hiring a practiced hand in the industry. Certainly, you can contract out the big stuff and plan on completing minor projects, such as installing annual beds, yourself. The choice is yours, and there are many options.

CAD KEY

A. Outbuilding
B. Large pond
C. Stepping stones
D. Hardscape patio
E. Outdoor kitchen area
F. Brick paver walkway
G. Picnic seating

CHAPTER 2

Handle with Care

The time you spend outdoors improving your property is a long-term investment. Of course, you immediately earn the pleasure of enjoying a space you molded with your own two hands. You'll increase your property value, and improve the aesthetics of your environment. Looks *do* matter, at least when landscaping is concerned. Second looks from others are even better!

But your work isn't finished when projects are complete.

You now graduate to the next phase of every project: care and upkeep. This is the to-be-continued of every project, the phase that will test your commitment to maintaining curb appeal. You know how your bathroom looks if you neglect clean-up for weeks—same goes for your kitchen, or any part of your house. Your outdoor living room, your landscape, deserves the same attention. When you stay on top of activities, such as trimming, watering, fertilizing, pruning, and general clean-up, the yard "work" will demand little of your time.

We'll discuss some basic care practices here, but it's a not a bad idea to brush up on maintenance foundation principles. Consider picking up a copy of *John Deere Landscaping and Lawn Care* if you want to dig deeper into lawn care practices.

For now, here's a crash course in maintenance to help you keep your landscape looking its best, year-round.

For example, your vibrant perennial display will need water to bloom, and you'll want to trim back bushes so they look tidy and stay within the bed lines you created for them. The four key maintenance activities are:

- **Mowing your lawn**
- **Watering turf and plants**
- **Fertilizing and protecting your lawn**
- **Trimming, edging, and pruning**

Ready to work? It's not that bad—promise! In fact, you'll likely enjoy the time you spend doting on your finished projects.

Never operate mowing equipment with the discharge shoot raised, removed, or altered, unless using a grass catcher. This device is designed to reduce the chance of thrown objects.

Mowing Know-How

There's more to mowing than making tall grass short. A proper cut will promote turf growth, discourage weeds and disease, and protect soil from losing moisture. Whether you operate a walk-behind or riding mower, the best cut is only possible with attention to timing, cutting height, terrain challenges, and safety.

Assuming you understand how to operate your mower, and have read the safety guidelines (where you'll find most troubleshooting answers), let's walk through each of these key points.

Timing: First of all, simply setting aside the time to mow is exhausting for some of us. Assuming you choose to maintain your own property, you'll have to approach mowing with a bit of flexibility. Just because Saturday morning is the most convenient time to mow doesn't mean it's the best time, especially if Friday night's downpour left puddles in your front yard. For safety and turf health reasons, don't mow when grass is wet. Mower wheels mat down turf and leave visible tracks. These stressed areas will not welcome sunlight, and disease likes dark, wet places. Also avoid mowing after sundown, when low visibility inhibits your ability to operate equipment safely. Hazards tend to blend in with the landscape when it's dark.

Cutting height: Aim to cut off just the top third of turf in a single pass. The recommended height for your lawn depends on turfgrass variety. If your turf is Kentucky Bluegrass, the recommended cutting height is 1½ to 3 inches (3.8 to 7.6 cm).

Case in point: You go on vacation for two weeks, return home, and your lawn looks like a prairie with turf exceeding 7 inches (17.8 cm). Considering the one-third rule, you'll need to mow your lawn a couple of times to achieve the recommended height. Set your cutting deck to remove 2 inches (5 cm) the first pass. Then mow again in the opposite direction, removing another 2 inches (5 cm). The result is 3 inch (7.6 cm) -long turf: right on the mark.

The reason you should only cut off one-third of your turf at one time is because when grass that is too long is lopped off and lays on the surface, it blocks sunlight and oxygen from penetrating the lawn. If you're cutting off one-third at a time, the clippings will decompose much easier, and actually add a layer of beneficial, organic compounds to turf. You may also choose to bag or rake clippings and compost them. *(See Compost Technique on page 60.)*

Terrain challenges: Most lawns aren't perfect squares or smooth as fresh asphalt. Ruts, slopes, and curvy bed lines are a reality for most of us. We must handle these obstacles with care, especially when operating a riding mower.

- If a tight angle compromises your safety, use a trimmer in that area, or choose a walk-behind for closer control.
- Increase the radius around trees by first using a line trimmer to cut grass close to the perimeter.
- If you must mow between two beds that don't allow room for equipment to pass through, consider using a walk-behind mower or trimmer for the job.
- Mow across slopes when using zero-turn and walk-behind mowers. Mow directly up and down slopes when operating a riding mower. To test if a slope is too steep to mow with a riding mower, try backing straight up the hill. If you can't mow a slope in forward using a riding mower, do not mow it with this equipment.
- Always avoid sudden stops or turns when mowing slopes.
- Mow slowly and always look behind you when moving in reverse.

Safety: Always read your operator's manual before mowing; and it's a good idea to review this information each year. Always clear the mowing area of debris—branches, children's toys, you name it; if it's not grass, it's a hazard. Also, explain to younger children that while mowers look fun to operate, they are not toys. Never give your child a ride on the mower. A great resource for safety tips is www.knowbeforeyoumow.com. Share this information with your family, and bookmark the site.

Switch mowing directions every week. Grass has a tendency to lay the way you mow it. When you alternate mowing directions, turf stands at attention, which allows for a cleaner cut.

QUICK TIP

If your soil doesn't readily accept water, its clay composition can be aired out with annual aeration. (See project on page 46). Aeration will speed up the percolation rate, which is how fast water soaks into the soil and reaches roots.

Water Works

Watering is generally the first task that comes to mind when discussing maintenance. Of course, plants need H_2O to grow. Certainly, turf will turn brown without moisture. Water is an essential element; we know this. But so often, we neglect to nourish the living components of our landscape. Why?

For one, gauging how much to water is more difficult than it seems. Concerned that we might not give our dear plants enough to drink, we overwater them in the process. Or, we react in the opposite manner and forget the watering process all together. But plants, unfortunately, aren't self-watering—they don't come equipped with red lights that blink "empty." There is a happy medium. To answer the how-much-how-often question, whether watering turf or a container garden, you must tune in to these variables: plant variety, climate, and soil type.

Watering Turf

Is your soil mostly sandy or clay based? Soil type will determine the rate at which water soaks into the soil. You can think of soil as a filter that water must pass through to reach grass roots. When soil is sandy and porous, water soaks in quickly, sometimes so quickly that roots don't have time to absorb moisture. Sandy soils will require deep watering to ensure water reaches roots.

When soil is mostly clay, you'll notice puddles forming on the ground surface as water gradually, slowly seeps into the earth. While water takes longer to soak into clay soils, this composition retains moisture longer, which is beneficial in the long run, because turf plants can survive drought periods. Water clay soils more frequently, for shorter periods of time.

Soil type is one watering variable, but it doesn't overrule turf variety or climate. Find out what type of turf your lawn contains, and learn the water needs for this variety. Your best bet is to play the meteorologist of your property and apply some good common sense. Are you expecting a heavy rain in the afternoon? Then avoid watering in the early morning. Has the weather been

Not sure whether you are watering enough? Buy a rain gauge at a garden center, and set it in turf, a garden, or a plant bed to find out how much water the space receives each week. To measure water application in a large area, space out rain gauges throughout the area.

Water conservation practices are always a good habit, whether you live in a desert climate where water is a luxury, or your weather forecast never fails to bring several days of showers a week. Consider these tips to conserve water:

- Mow your lawn at a higher than normal height
- Avoid applying growth-promoting fertilizer
- Control thatch and soil compaction so water soaks in efficiently
- Do not allow water to run off on to sidewalks or driveways

exceptionally dry? Account for this in your watering program. Most of all, follow this rule of thumb: Water early in the morning. That way, moisture will absorb into soil and reach roots before the sun evaporates it.

Watering Plants

Plant tags provide need-to-know details on plants' water requirements. Read these before installing plants, and group together varieties with similar water needs. In plant beds, a layer of mulch will help soil retain moisture, especially during dry times or hot days with intense sun.

Like turf, you'll want to water plant beds and gardens in early morning to avoid evaporation and disease development. If you water at night, and moisture sits, marinating for hours until morning, you will create an attractive environment for fungus and unwanted insects. Meanwhile, overly moist soil does not allow oxygen and nutrients to reach roots. They'll respond by rotting, not at all what you intended to accomplish with a water "night cap."

Drip irrigation can ease the burden of watering potted plants, gardens, and beds. (Learn how to install it on page 48.) But as a general rule, you should water plants until you notice moisture has absorbed and the area has dried out. Then, apply another dose of water. Continue in this manner until you have applied the appropriate amount of water, which depends on the plant variety. (Again, read those labels!) For containers, you can water until you notice drips percolating from drainage holes in the bottom of the pot. This is an obvious sign that moisture is reaching the root zone.

THE BEST TIME to water is early morning to avoid combating water loss from hot, daytime sun.

Plant Food & Disease Prevention

Because we often encourage turf and plants to grow in challenging conditions, whether in extreme climates or challenging terrain, they need extra nutrients to achieve the vitality and longevity we expect. Think of fertilizer and related lawn care products as vitamins for your turf. You may choose to hire a certified lawn care professional to manage this portion of your maintenance. This is not a bad idea, as timing and applying the correct rate of product per square inch do require a bit of homework. We'll discuss the intricacies of fertilizer application on page 52.

In the meantime, here are some basics you'll want to build into your plant and turf nutrition program:

Slow-release fertilizer: Feeds plants gradually over a period of time, and keeps flowers from starving, too.

Herbicides: Weed control products are available in several forms: selective, nonselective, contact, and systemic. Selective herbicides knock down certain weed species without affecting the growth of other plants. Most herbicides are selective. Nonselective herbicides wipe out all green plants. Use these if you plan to re-establish turf or create a new plant bed. Also use non-selective products to clear weeds from sidewalk and driveway cracks. Contact herbicides are spot treatments that only affect the area touched by the formula. These generally require repeat applications.

Pesticides and insecticides: These products target specific lawn care issues, and many homeowners choose to reserve these services for professionals, who can accurately identify disease and insect problems and prepare a treatment plan.

The Trimmings

Shrubs, trees, and turf all need touch-up work throughout the season to sustain a polished finish. You'll achieve neat lines by clipping, pruning, edging, and trimming. So think of yourself as a landscape barber. Split ends are messy, as is ragged turf that spills over the lawn border onto sidewalks. An uneven haircut looks like a mistake, and so do shrubs that are bald on one side as a casualty of overpruning. Your goal is to keep up curb appeal year-round, to really maximize the impact of the projects you complete. By taking care of "the trimmings," you can do just that.

Whether you're edging your lawn, or trimming back an unruly shrub, make this your mantra: Less is more. Your lawn edge should not look like a step down from the rest of the yard. If you mow at 3 inches (7.6 cm), trim edges at 3 inches (7.6 cm). Likewise, unless your landscape design includes topiaries, which we'll address on page 112, aim for a natural finish. Select individual, stray branches from shrubs and clip them with hand shears or pruning shears. Hedge trimmers tempt most of us to swipe over the top of shrubs and deliver a flat-top cut that's too short.

Examine shrubs and prune those with unruly growth, weakened or dead branches, disease-infected branches and leaves, or crossing branches. Conservatively removing growth is beneficial to plant health by improving light penetration, and allowing sun and air to circulate. When you remove dead, weakened, and disease-infected branches, you prolong the useful life of the plant. Finally, you'll keep your landscape looking neat and clean. Learn more in our Tree & Shrub Pruning Clinic on page 36. (See—we've got lots of ideas for you!)

CHAPTER 3

Tools of the Trade

As you master the projects in this book, you'll gradually begin to build up your arsenal of tools, planting supplies, and power equipment. A supplies list in every chapter will help you gather the essentials for completing projects. Many of these tools you'll find in your garage already, while others are more specialized. Remember, you can always rent power saws, trenchers, power augers, plate compactors, and other implements you'll only use occasionally.

When you invest in equipment or tools, refer to consumer guides and talk to a specialist at your hardware or supply store. You want sturdy, long-lasting tools, so get a handle on them before making a purchase. Check grips for comfort, and be sure that the tool size is comfortable. For the tools you will use most often, like spades, shovels, and trowels, buy the highest quality you can afford. A good garden spade may last twenty to thirty years. When purchasing power equipment for lawn maintenance (mowers, edgers, trimmers), buy from an authorized dealer who will help you choose the correct machine for your application, and also service the equipment and supply extra parts.

FOR THE TOOLS you'll use all the time, invest in the highest quality you can: rubber mallet (A), small maul (B), large maul (C), square shovel (D), garden shovel (E), carpenter's level (F), garden rake (G), circular saw (H), garden hose (I).

GARDENING BASICS

- Spade
- Hoe
- Garden trowel
- Garden or bow rake
- Garden hose
- Plant stakes
- Spading or garden fork
- Bypass pruner
- Anvil pruner

GARDENING EXTRAS

- Power tiller
- Cultivator

LAWN AND LANDSCAPING BASICS

- Mower
- Trimmer
- Edger
- Hedge shears
- Wheelbarrow
- Shovel
- Leaf rake
- Loppers
- Pruning saw
- Sprinkler

LAWN AND LANDSCAPING EXTRAS

- String trimmer
- Power edger
- Handheld blower
- Drop or rotary spreader
- Hand pump sprayer
- Hand maul
- Line level
- Hand tamp

CARPENTRY BASICS

- Hammer
- Power drill
- Screwdriver
- Level
- Tape measure
- Carpenter's square
- Circular saw
- Adjustable wrench

TOOLS TO RENT

- Jackhammer
- Power auger
- Plate compactor
- Reciprocating saw
- Aerator
- Chain saw
- Chipper
- Pressure washer

INVEST IN A QUALITY cordless drill (A), and rent other equipment you'll only use occasionally such as a cordless reciprocating saw (B), jigsaw (C).

PLANTING SUPPLIES

Most of the projects in the Plants & Gardens portion of this book require these supplies.

- Gardener's gloves
- Kneeler
- Garden trowel
- Spading or garden fork
- Spade
- Hand pruners
- Watering can
- Measuring tape

THIS WALK-BEHIND mower is ideal for most residential properties. Riding mowers will accommodate larger lawns.

PART TWO

Landscape & Lawn Care

Your backyard is a living canvas. You add the colors and features; you infuse your personality and invent an outdoor living environment, one project at a time. But before you can embellish, you must prime your canvas. You need a strong foundation: healthy trees, lush grass, and crisp bed edges. The lawn care and landscape best practices outlined in this section will prepare your property for the projects to come.

PROJECT

Repair a Dead Spot

We've all experienced turf casualties.
Blame it on the dog, the kids, a battle with disease, a dry
spell. For whatever reason, a spot of grass gave up and
turned brown. Whether the dead zone is in the middle
of your front yard or tucked in a backyard corner, the
notion that a select population of grass will not respond
to your doting applications of fertilizer and extra douses
of water is frustrating. The strawlike, matted spot is like
a blank stare: What are you going to do about it?

The repair process is painless, though it requires
patience while new turf grows in. Follow these steps,
and learn how to fill in that stubborn, brown blemish
in your yard. The rest of your lawn is lush and inviting.
Don't let a little dead spot spoil it.

The Dirt

For any number of reasons, a spot of turf can die out
and not respond to typical turf-care stimulants like
fertilizer and water. If your pet has a preferred "area,"
don't expect grass to thrive. Also, heavy foot traffic can
wear away spots of your lawn, as can chemical burn or
an isolated weed or disease infestation. Determine the
cause of the bare spot so you will not have repeat repairs
each season.

Similar Seed

When reseeding, your goal is to achieve a seamless
transition from the patched spot to the rest of the lawn.
You'll want to match the seed with existing turfgrass.
This is a challenge for many of us, especially with new
construction. With so many turf grass blends on the
market today, who's to know whether the lawn is a
"contractor's mix" or a fine fescue with a bit of perennial ryegrass on the side? Ask a university extension if
you question the variety of your turf. Or, call a lawn care
professional, who can identify the type.

Preliminaries

Treat this dead spot as you would a blank slate—a mini lawn. Though the area you are working with is decidedly smaller, establishing healthy soil and nourishing turfgrass seedlings is just as important in a footprint-sized space as on a large property.

Supplies

- **Spade**
- **Tamper (optional)**
- **Topsoil**
- **Turfgrass seed**
- **Hay or paper mulch**

Steps

1. Remove the dead spot with a spade, digging straight down into the ground. Dig as deep as necessary to remove all the soil containing turf roots. Removing the damaged roots and clearing out the area will remove possible insect infestations or contamination.

2. Fill the hole with topsoil. Choose a loamy soil that will provide plenty of nutrients for new seeds to establish. Tamp down soil so it is level with the turf.

3. Seed the area with a mix that matches your existing turfgrass **(Figure 1)**.

4. Cover the area with hay or paper mulch product to protect it from losing moisture and to deter birds, which like to dine on seeds.

5. Water the spot and take care to keep the area moist for the few first weeks, while seeds germinate and sprout.

Figure 1

PROJECT

Tree & Shrub Pruning Clinic

Pruning can rejuvenate a plant, force new growth, and prolong the life of trees and shrubs, if properly executed. The entire plant benefits when you remove select portions, such as unruly shoots, damaged branches, or overbearing growth. Regular pruning will promote succulent, new growth; discourage disease; and improve plants' overall appearance.

Then there are space issues. How much real estate have you allotted for each shrub, every woody ornamental? Most of us don't have room to allow plants to grow untamed, and doing so isn't always the best choice for trees and shrubs with suffering branches.

Aesthetically speaking, some branches just need to go. Trim back bushes that reach over a heavy foot-traffic area. Removing this growth clears the path, ensuring safety. Also, pruning flowering trees and shrubs helps the plant produce stronger stems, more colorful berries, and vibrant flowers. (We'll explain why in Shrub Pruning Steps on page 39.)

Timing and technique are critical when pruning. There are various cuts and particulars to keep in mind before you begin snipping away.

The Dirt

Your pruning technique will, quite literally, mold the future of a shrub or tree. Pinch the ends off of plants for a bushy look. Restore an ornamental's natural shape with some clean-up cuts. Remove rubbing tree branches, where abrasion becomes an open wound for disease to enter. The trick to properly pruning trees and shrubs is to always remember: less is more.

YOU'LL NEED LOPPERS and pruners to manage most pruning jobs.

That rule in mind, step back from the shrub you are about to prune. Examine its natural shape. Which way do branches grow? Is the shrub top-heavy, with umbrella-like growth that prevents lower branches from soaking in sunlight? Correct pruning is selective and intentional. Following are steps to achieve various types of pruning cuts, and instructions on when these cuts are appropriate.

Supplies

You'll need different tools for trees and shrubs. And depending on the type of pruning you want to accomplish, you may reach for hand pruners or electric hedge trimmers. Read the steps carefully before deciding which of the following cutting tools is the best option for your application.

- **Pruning knife**
- **Hand pruner**
- **Hedge clippers**
- **Lopper**
- **Bow saw**
- **Pruning saw**
- **Pole saw**
- **Hedge trimmer**
- **Chain saw**

Preliminaries

Light, corrective pruning (less than 10 percent of the tree or shrub canopy) can be done all year. But when more severe cuts, such as heading back, thinning, or rejuvenation are concerned, timing is critical. Essentially, you want to prune when plants are under the least amount of stress. That way, trees and shrubs will heal successfully from wounds that shears and clippers inevitably cause. Stress means flowering, growing, or any activity related to the plant life cycle.

For this reason, late winter and early spring are the best times to conduct severe pruning in most woody plants. Late-summer pruning primes shrubs for growth at the wrong time: right before harsh weather. New growth may not have time to develop to withstand the cold, therefore increasing susceptibility to disease.

Figure 1

Figure 2

Don't wait until a plant has outgrown a space before pruning it. Adopt the practice as part of your routine maintenance regimen. Be on the lookout for plants with dead, dying, or diseased wood. These are easy entries for insects and disease that can spread.

Follow the same rule for flowering trees and shrubs. Summer-flowering shrubs should be pruned before new growth begins. Shoot for late winter or early spring. On the other hand, if you snip off spring-blooming bud tips in the fall or winter, you'll remove flower buds that are waiting to pop. Without them, your shrub will lose its flower power. Prune spring-bloomers immediately after flowers fade in late spring, and before the Fourth of July.

Shrub Pruning Steps

There are several types of pruning, and ideally, you'll use a combination of these methods.

Pinching: The terminal of a shoot is the tip of the stem (the green portion before it becomes woody). The terminal produces a hormone that prevents lateral buds from developing. When you remove the terminal, this hormone-producing bud is lost, allowing lateral buds to grow. Pinching reduces the length of a shoot and promotes filler, or side growth. Pinch off especially long shoots from inside the shrub canopy **(Figure 1)**.

HEDGE TRIMMERS like these are convenient tools for shearing branches. This practice is reserved for formal landscape designs.

IMPROVING BRANCH HEALTH

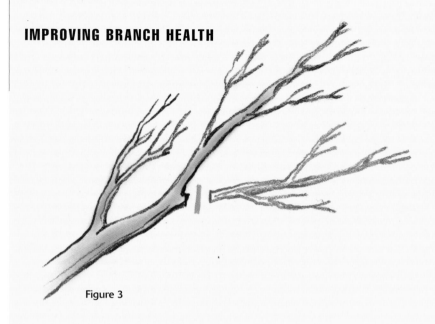

Figure 3

MAKING THE RIGHT CUT

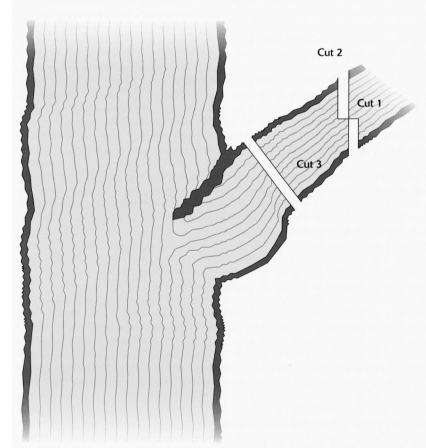

TO PREVENT DAMAGE, larger tree branches should be cut in three steps. Cuts one and two remove the main weight of the branch. Cut three must be just outside the branch collar at a slight angle.

Heading Back: You can increase the density of a tree or shrub by cutting terminal shoots back to a healthy branch or bud. Manipulate the shape of the shrub by cutting inward or outward growing shoots. Be sure that the top bud is located on the side of the branch that faces the direction you want it to grow. For example, an inward-facing bud will develop into a branch that reaches into the canopy. If you allow two opposite-facing buds to grow, the result is a weak, Y-shaped branch. So choose your growth direction, and then remove buds accordingly **(Figure 2,** page 38**)**.

Thinning: Target the oldest, tallest stems first when thinning, which is cutting branches off from the parent stem. (You'll reach into the shrub canopy to accomplish this successfully.) Prune branches that are one-third the diameter of the parent stem. To better visualize where to cut, imagine the Y junction where a lateral branch meets the parent stem **(Figure 3).** As with all pruning cuts, practice moderation.

Rejuvenation: Remove the oldest branches by leaving little but a stub near the ground. Young branches can also be cut back, as well as thin stems.

Shearing: Using hedge trimmers, a swipe over the top of a shrub, which removes the terminal and most shoots, will give you a formal, topiary look. Shearing, by no means, produces a natural look; and clean angles must be clipped back throughout the summer to maintain the shape. Shearing is not necessarily beneficial, because it forces growth on the exterior of the plant, which blocks light and oxygen from the center. You're left with a shell of a shrub—leaves on the outside, naked branches on the inside.

THINNING THE TREE CANOPY

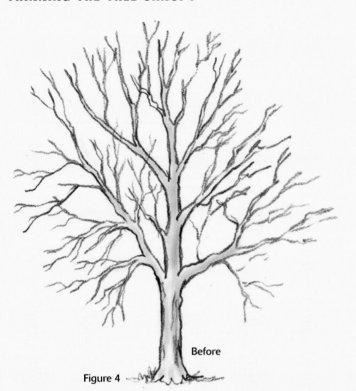

Before

Figure 4

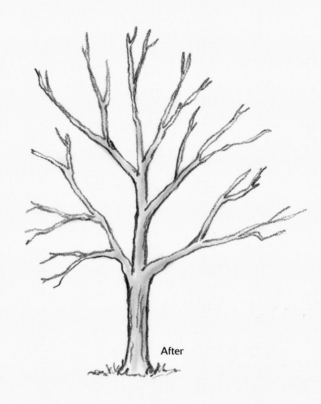

After

Tree Pruning Steps

Always prune tree branches by cutting just outside the tree collar (*See Making the Right Cut, page 40.*) You'll notice a circular closure around the wound as the tree begins to heal.

Thinning: These cuts reduce the tree canopy and allow wind to pass through branches. Thinning is a safety measure if you are concerned a storm will damage a tree and surrounding property. Remove dead, broken, weak, and diseased branches. Cut them back to their point of origin or to laterals that are at least one-third the diameter of the branch you are removing. Be sure to remove less than 25 percent of foliage at one time. It's best to thin trees in the winter, when they are dormant **(Figure 4).**

Heading Back: If your goal is to reduce the size of your tree, cut back lateral branches and head tips of laterals.

Reduction Cut: Most common in younger trees, these cuts remove an offshoot branch back to a thicker branch attached to the tree trunk. Pictured (opposite) is a cut to remove a perpendicular branch.

PROJECT PAIRINGS

NOW THAT YOUR SHRUBS are shipshape, try these projects:

Install Bed Edging   128
Want to contain your shrubs? Bed edging will do the trick.

Operation Conceal   190
Shrubs and trees are nature's privacy fences.

PROJECT

Transplant Trees & Shrubs

Sometimes, finding space for new landscape features requires relocating existing elements. Perhaps a favorite tree outgrew its humble spot or a trio of shrubs must be uprooted to accommodate a patio. Even if you are moving to a new home, you can still preserve a piece of your former landscape.

But it's not as easy as it sounds. Transplanting trees and shrubs requires hard labor, especially for mature plants with developed root systems, which extend well beyond a tree's drip line. Before you make the decision to find new real estate for a beloved tree, ensure that that your property contains a new spot that will accommodate its light, soil, and space needs.

The Dirt

Successful transplantation requires a bit of math. You must know the diameter of the trunk, which will help you determine how much of the root ball to remove. You can find the diameter by measuring around the trunk (the circumference) and dividing that number by 3.14. If your tree or shrub has a trunk that is smaller than 1 inch (7.6 cm) in diameter, you will not need to relocate a solid root ball. But chances are, if you are truly attached to a tree, enough time has passed that it is beyond this nimble stage. You'll need to remove the plant's root ball, and this will involve quite a bit of digging.

Here's exactly how much:

The general rule is to dig a 10 to 12 inch (25.4 to 30.5 cm) root ball for every 1 inch (2.5 cm) of trunk diameter. To move a tree that is 3 inches (7.6 cm) in diameter, you must dig a root ball that is 30 to 36 inches (76.2 to 91.4 cm) in diameter.

Prime Location

You may choose to transplant a tree because it isn't thriving in the current location. By moving it to a spot where soil or light is more desirable, for example, you can give the tree a new lease on life. Otherwise, pick an area of your property with light and soil qualities that are similar to the current location of the tree or shrub. You should test the soil pH of the desired location. A university extension can assist you with this process. Also, be sure to position the tree so it is facing the same direction where it received adequate air and light. Tie a marker around one of the branches before you move the tree. That way, you can reposition the tree correctly in the new spot.

BEFORE MOVING A TREE, you want to train feeder roots to develop closer to the trunk. This is accomplished by root pruning.

Prepare with Root Pruning

The season prior to transplanting a tree, you should prune the roots. The best time to transplant is in the fall, late winter, or early spring before buds break. That said, if you plan to transplant the tree in the spring, perform root pruning in the fall, after leaves drop. The point of root pruning is to stimulate new feeder roots closer to the trunk. You see, trees actually feed quite far away from the trunk. When you transplant the tree, you want to preserve feeder roots that absorb moisture so the tree will adapt well to the new location.

The process is like performing a partial transplantation, without actually digging up the tree.

- **Start by watering soil** the day before pruning.
- **Mark the pruning area,** referring to the diameter rule (page 42) to determine the circumference around the tree where you will dig a trench, therefore cutting the roots.
- **Cut a trench** along the marked area, digging down about 2 feet (0.6 m) using a sharp spade. Use pruners or loppers to cut roots as you trench, if necessary. Do not dig underneath the tree. You are pruning, not removing the root ball.
- **Replace soil** and add water.

Preliminaries

Before you move the tree or shrub, dig and prepare the new hole. Dig the hole wider, but not deeper than the root ball you want to transplant. This is important because if the hole is too deep for the root ball, and it sinks down so the top of the ball is below ground level, water will collect in this low zone. The net result could be root rot, and this disease may not set in for a number of years. By that time, saving the plant is near impossible. So err on the shallow side of digging.

Ultimately, you want to create a welcome home for the tree, so be sure to moisten the hole before transplanting. That way, roots will not go into shock when you set them into their new environment.

Supplies

- **Measuring tape**
- **Spade**
- **Shovel**
- **Loppers and pruners**
- **Rope (to tie back low branches)**
- **Tarp or burlap**
- **Mulch**
- **Stakes**

Resist the temptation to use your shovel to break up the ground at the bottom of the new hole. Loose soil does not encourage roots to adapt better to the new location. Actually, the root ball may sink into the ground, promote water collection, and eventually cause root rot.

Steps

1. Water the soil the day before to reduce stress to plant roots.

2. Dig the new planting hole and moisten it with water.

3. Gently remove topsoil and mark the area you will remove according to the measurements describe on page 42. You will cut a trench 4 to 6 inches (10.2 to 15.2 cm) outside of the area you root pruned. This ensures you include all root feeders in the ball you will transplant.

4. Using a spade, dig progressively deeper, shaping the root ball. Cut large roots with loppers or pruners. Once you reach the correct depth, begin digging underneath the root ball.

5. Place a tarp or piece of burlap into the hole on one side of the root ball. Dig under the ball, cutting roots away from the earth, and tilt the ball onto the tarp for moving. Never lift the plant by its trunk; ease it out of the ground by lifting it up from underneath. The tarp will protect the root ball.

6. You can transport the tree to its new location by dragging the tarp with the tree on it. Or, in cases where you will move the tree to a different address (a new home, for example), wrap the tree in burlap so it can "breathe" but stays protected. Lay the tree on its side and transport it in a truck bed or vehicle that can accommodate the tree size.

7. Replace soil and lay ring of mulch around the new transplant.

8. Plant care is critical after moving a tree or shrub. Watering requirements will depend on the soil texture and temperature, and the needs of the specific plant variety. Deep watering will ensure that water reaches roots. You can expect that your transplant will need months, or several years for mature plants, for full recovery.

PROJECT PAIRINGS

YOU RELOCATED YOUR TREE, now what?

Repair a Dead Spot   36
Revitalize the area you dug up with this spot-treatment project.

Ground Cover   84
Transplanting a tree disrupts the surrounding turf area. You may consider planting an alternative to grass.

PROJECT

Aerate Your Lawn

After the growing season, your yard could probably use a breather. Rapid root growth and foot traffic can compact soil, which cuts off oxygen and nutrient supply. Consider what your yard looks like beneath the grass. Soil is an underground subway of roots, all vying for oxygen, nutrients, and water. Compact soil strains roots ability to absorb these essentials and grow strong. Meanwhile, turf plants that depend on these roots don't get the food they need. Grass turns brown and wilts.

The solution is to aerate. Aeration literally airs out the earth and unplugs the ground by mild agitation with an aerator machine. The aerator punctures the ground with a coring tool, removing test-tube sized cylinders of soil. Removing these vial-sized plugs of soil and turf restores air and water circulation to roots, and makes room for new growth come spring.

The time to aerate is fall, if you have cool-season grass. The process is no more complicated than mowing your lawn. But as with mowing, there are care practices that will help you maximize the benefits of aeration.

The Dirt

You might question whether you should aerate your lawn. How do you tell if your soil is clogged? Not to worry. There are signs that will help you recognize whether your turf could use a breath of fresh air. And before you refuse the service from your lawn care service, or resist renting a machine to do it yourself, you should know that you really can't harm your lawn by aerating it. The most important rule to remember is to aerate when your lawn is the least stressed out. Fall is best for cool-season lawns. For warm-season turf, May through August is peak aerating season. Warm-season grasses repair more quickly from mild agitation in summer, when they are strongest.

S.O.S.—Save Our Soil

The signs that your turf needs to be aerated are often subtle. Here are some clues:

YOU CAN RENT an aerator machine for the day, and do the job yourself.

Balding Turf: Compacted soil prevents root systems from developing. You might notice patches where grass isn't as dense.

Matted-down Grass: Compacted soil tends to retain moisture longer—too long in some cases. Roots can begin to rot, resulting in a weak turf plant that doesn't stand up straight.

Sparse New Growth: Weak roots and turf don't fill in to be a dense, lush carpet of grass. Compacted soil basically chokes roots and cuts off their oxygen and nutrient supply, inhibiting turf growth.

Pools of Water: In severe cases, you'll notice that pools of water collect on your lawn and moisture does not easily absorb into soil. This is a sign that the lawn is compacted and does not have pores to absorb water.

Tough Ground: Can you push a screwdriver or similar tool into the ground easily, or do you feel like you're driving metal into rock? If the latter is true, you better aerate.

Agitated, but Healthy

Why agitate your turf? It sounds like a bad thing, doesn't it? Actually, stirring up the soil to make room for new growth is exactly what your lawn may need after a growing season or two. The reason is compaction. Compaction occurs slowly over time, and environmental stressors are often the cause. Foot traffic compresses soil, and equipment bears weight on the ground. Your lawnmower is the number one offender. While pressure certainly is not fatal to turf, daily activities and lawn maintenance gradually compact soil.

Meanwhile, roots grow full-throttle in summer and fill in space underground. Upstairs, at the surface, your lawn looks thick and rich. But by the end of the growing season, roots are crowded, turf is tired, and your soil is hard concrete. This means it is not welcoming water or oxygen: a death sentence for turf.

But, stir up the soil a bit—unplug it, clear out its pores—and you'll make room for nutrients and oxygen to sink into the soil.

Preliminaries

You can rent an aerator for a reasonable price. If your neighbors are on the same lawn care schedule, round up a crew and split the cost for the day. This project won't take more than a couple of hours. If you rent a machine, ask the retailer for a quick lesson before taking it home. Aerators aren't difficult to operate, but since you only run them once a year, a refresher course can't hurt.

Before you begin, be sure soil is somewhat moist, but not drenched. A little moisture will soften the ground and allow the core cutter to work efficiently; too much moisture and you will turn your lawn into a mud pie. Also, be sure to clear your yard of any debris. Mark irrigation system heads, pet tie-ups, and other stakes or fixtures in the ground. The corers on aerator machines are unforgiving, and even strong hardware will probably not survive the puncturing force.

Supplies
- **Lawn rake (for removing debris)**
- **Core aerator machine**

Steps

1. Be sure your lawn is the right moisture level and temperature for aerating. If necessary, water your lawn the day before so you don't overwork equipment by forcing core cutters to drive into rock-hard soil.

2. Most core aerators are self-propelled. Make even passes across the lawn as if you are mowing the area.

3. You may choose to rake up cores to avoid squashing them back into the lawn; or you can allow them to dry up and the material will return to turf and serve as a valuable nitrogen and nutrient source.

4. Be sure to water your lawn after aerating. Because one purpose of creating pores in soil is to allow water and oxygen to enter the ground, give your lawn a good soak so roots can drink up moisture and begin the rebuilding process.

YOU MAY CHOOSE to rake up soil plugs to avoid squashing them back into the lawn, or you can allow them to dry up and dissipate; plugs are a source of nitrogen and nutrients to soil.

PROJECT

Install Drip Irrigation

As you color your landscape with decadent flower beds and create container gardens teeming with plants, you're probably wondering if you can also install insurance to protect your hard work! Actually, the best way to preserve plantings is to feed them regularly. Makes sense, right? Proper watering practices are critical for a landscape to grow and thrive; how to deliver a steady amount of water that plant beds need on a consistent basis tends to stump even avid gardeners.

Most of us are guilty of one of these watering habits: We set and forget sprinkler systems; we remember an occasional douse with a watering can; or, confident in Mother Nature's ability to do the job without help, we ignore the chore of watering all together. None of these methods will benefit your landscape.

Thankfully, technology, and an array of easy-to-install irrigation products on the market, can alleviate the burden of watering. We'll show you how to install a drip irrigation system yourself—it's easy. And you'll save yourself the worry of over watering. (How many times have you asked yourself, after pulling out of the driveway, whether you left a sprinkler running or completely forget to turn it on?)

The Dirt

Drip irrigation, in particular, ensures that plants get a gradual, deep soak. Drip systems look like garden hoses with emitters (nozzles) that protrude from the tubing. These emitters deliver water to targeted areas, such as specific plants in a bed. Drip irrigation systems work much like a water fountain with no pressure. Water trickles from emitters and slowly seeps into soil.

The benefit of drip irrigation is that you don't get the runoff you might with higher-powered sprinkler systems or by hand watering with a garden hose. Also, drip irrigation is ideal for containers and plant beds because you can position emitters according to plant placement, or snake hoses throughout beds to ensure even water coverage.

Drip Applications

Drip irrigation isn't designed to water your lawn, but it is ideal in the following applications:

- **Plant and flower beds**
- **Vegetable gardens**
- **Container plantings**
- **Beds with trees and ornamentals**

All you need to support a drip system is an outdoor spigot. You can purchase tubing in various lengths and widths, and kits contain connectors and emitters, which allow you to customize the system so it delivers water based on plant placement. For example, you can cut and split hose into sections, or arrange it along curvy beds. Because you choose the exact placement, you'll conserve resources while watering. You can drain as much as 400 gallons (1514 L) of water per hour from the water table by using a hose. This is far more liquid than your soil will accept, especially if it is primarily composed of clay.

Go Deep with Drip

Agronomists preach the importance of deep-root watering. This practice ensures moisture penetrates the surface and sinks into soil, where roots can soak it up and benefit from its nutrients. Drip irrigation achieves this. When you water with a hose, you will notice that puddles begin to form. These may eventually grow into miniature lakes, branch off into streams, and run off into other areas of your landscape, causing erosion. Meanwhile, standing water can suffocate young flowers and plants, preventing oxygen from reaching roots. Plants overwhelmed by water are more susceptible to disease.

The solution is to install a drip irrigation system, which will allow you to feed flowers and plants gradually. Think of it as serving them minimeals throughout the day. Plants can metabolize, or soak in, the water. Also, because drip irrigation delivers water drop by drop, moisture won't displace oxygen, and roots will receive both vital nutrients.

Preliminaries

You can purchase different types of tubing for drip irrigation. It is measured by the inside diameter (of the hose) and the outside diameter. This is important to note, especially if you are adding on sections of tubing to an existing drip system. Be sure to purchase the correct size tubing and a coupling system to join the sections. Also, measure the space where you'll install the system before purchasing a drip hose or kit. You don't want to run out of materials midproject.

The hose-end drip system we'll show you how to install is a kit, which you can purchase at garden stores or retail outlets. It contains tubing, emitters, and couplers. Be sure to read the manufacturer's directions before beginning the project.

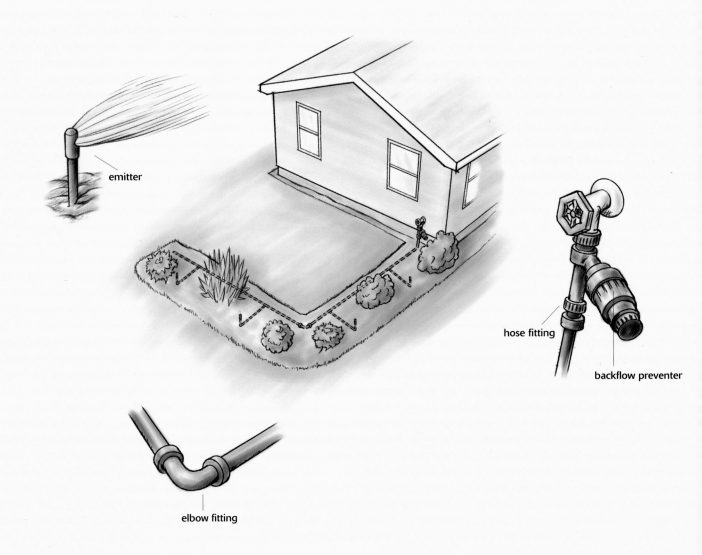

emitter

hose fitting

backflow preventer

elbow fitting

Soaker hoses are a form of drip irrigation. They "weep" water from tiny holes along the length of the hose, with a 2 to 3 inch (5.1 to 7.6 cm) watering width (depending on soil conditions). You can set them on the ground or bury them under mulch. Cut hose to desired length, and use end caps or hose fittings as needed.

Supplies
- **Filter**
- **Backflow preventer**
- **Hose fitting**
- **Tee fittings, elbow fittings, and couplers**
- **Support stakes**
- **End fittings**

Steps

1. Measure and cut tubing to fit the area.

2. Fit tubing into elbow-shaped joints, which will allow you to run a system along corners and to arrange tubing in a row formation for watering vegetable gardens or flower beds.

3. Attach the filter and backflow preventer to the water source. If the water pressure is more than 50 psi, you'll need a pressure regulator.

4. Some kits contain emitters that allow you to control where the water will spray from the tubing. Think of them as mini-irrigation spray heads. Puncture emitters into tubing according to instructions on the packaging. Be sure to align emitters, so they deliver water to desired plants.

Follow the manufacturer's directions for draining the irrigation system in cold winter climates.

PROJECT PAIRINGS

NOW THAT YOUR SYSTEM IS INSTALLED, try these complementary projects:

Compost Technique   60
Aside from water, soil nutrition is also critical to plant health.

Container Planting Clinic   104
Think of these as portable plant beds.

Install Landscape Lighting   184
Turn on nightlights so you can enjoy beds twenty four/seven

PROJECT

Fertilizer Application Clinic

Fertilizer is plant nutrition, and when applied at the correct rate with careful technique, you'll enhance the appearance and vigor of your lawn. We'll walk you through steps so you can determine the type of fertilizer to buy, how much to apply, and when are the most critical times for cool- and warm-season grasses to get their vitamins.

The Dirt

Before you head outdoors, you should understand how fertilizer works so you can choose the proper mix for your property, and apply it at the appropriate time.

N-P-K: What Does It Mean?

The essential elements of fertilizer are nitrogen, phosphorus, and potassium, otherwise known as N, P, and K. (Remember these abbreviations from the periodic table of the elements in chemistry class?) Each plays a starring role in how fertilizer sparks green-up, promotes turf root growth, and helps turf survive through hard winters and hot summers.

Nitrogen is responsible for color. It helps turf plants metabolize and produce leaf growth. Nitrogen is quick-release or slow-release, which refers to fast-acting or long-term nitrogen activity. Ideally, purchase a fertilizer blend that contains both types of nitrogen.

Phosphorus promotes root growth. This is especially important for seedlings. If you are establishing cool-season grass, an application of fertilizer with higher phosphorus ratings will help your lawn mature more quickly. (Look for a larger middle number in the N-P-K rating on the bag.) Because phosphorus also promotes algae growth, many communities ban the sale and use of

fertilizers containing phosphorus. You can get a permit to apply phosphorus in these communities if a soil test proves a deficiency.

Potassium protects turf. It plays a strong role in sustaining turf during times of drought, and it prevents winterkill in some grasses. In cool-season lawns, a stronger dose of potassium in the fall will help your lawn endure winter, and emerge healthy come spring.

NITROGEN (A), PHOSPHORUS (B), and POTASSIUM (C) are key fertilizer ingredients.

Timing Is Everything

For optimum performance, plan on fertilizing your lawn several times during the growing season. Lighter, more frequent application rates ensure that grass gets regular, balanced meals when it needs the energy the most. Application timing varies according to your location and turf type.

COOL-SEASON GRASSES

Spring: Stimulate your lawn to promote growth. Avoid fertilizer blends with too much nitrogen, which will fast-forward growth and only result in more mowing work for you.

Summer: Do not overfertilize during the summer, when plants are under stress. A couple of light fertilizer applications will do the trick. Focus on maintenance and controlling weed, disease, and insect problems.

Fall: This is the most crucial time to fertilize cool-season grasses. Fall fertilization provides turf nutrients to store during dormancy, so it can endure the winter.

WARM-SEASON GRASSES

Spring: This is the most critical time to fertilize. Warm-season grasses need nutrients so they can grow strong during the hot summer. A slow-release fertilizer will prevent overly rapid growth during the peak season.

Summer: Apply frequent, light doses of fertilizer.

Fall: Ease up on fertilizer during this time, when warm-season grasses go dormant.

The Right Rate

For even fertilizer distribution, you must calibrate your spreader. Calibration is the process of setting your spreader to distribute granules at the recommended label rate. Here comes the math. To determine the right rate, measure your lawn with a wheel measure or estimate the size by stepping off the length and width. If the product label says the fertilizer will cover 5,000 square feet (464.5 square meters), and your property is 15,000 square feet (1,393.5 square meters), you will need three bags. You should always apply fertilizer in two applications: one horizontal pass with the spreader, followed by an application perpendicular to your first pass. So, for the property we described, you would apply 1½ bags of fertilizer on your first pass, and 1½ bags on the second, perpendicular pass.

Always read labels before purchasing and applying any lawn care product. All labels indicate the products N-P-K ratio, and they will explain how much fertilizer to apply. Labels also provide critical safety information, such as the necessity for eye protection and gloves with handling. Children and pets should not play in the yard following fertilizer application.

Signs of overfertilization include:
- **Plant leaves look succulent,** and blades appear full of moisture
- **Rubbing a blade** between your fingers stains hands green
- **Leaves flop over** and look heavy or less vigorous
- **Dense, green tufts grow** in areas that responded more readily to nitrogen content

Supplies
- **Broadcast spreader, also called a rotary spreader**
- **Granular fertilizer**

Steps

1. Be sure the spreader's release door is closed before filling the hopper with the appropriate amount of product, as indicated in The Right Rate. Always fill the spreader over a hard surface so you can sweep up spills.

2. Divide the application amount in half. Apply the first half in one direction, then apply the second half in a path perpendicular to your first pass. A double-pass method prevents striping patterns that result when you miss a spot.

3. While making straight passes across your lawn, similar to how you might mow grass, be sure to slightly overlap passes so you don't leave an untreated line of turf.

PROJECT PAIRINGS

COMPLEMENT YOUR HEALTHY, green lawn with these projects:

Install Drip Irrigation   48
Proper watering practices are a critical part of your lawn care regimen. Install a system so you don't forget to quench your turf's thirst.

Make Your Own Stepping Stones   126
Reduce foot traffic on your beautiful turf with inventive stepping stones.

Maximizing a Small Space   206
Small spaces deserve just as much attention. Try these big-impact ideas.

PROJECT

Edging Basics

Edging and trimming are finishing touches that mark the difference between a plain old mowed lawn and a manicured property. There's something about a crisp, clean edge that completes the look of any lawn. You can compare these tasks to coloring within the lines of a drawing. You may not notice why the finished product looks impressive, but you can certainly tell when a careless hand did not bother to erase messy work.

So don't short-cut your maintenance routine by leaving out the finishing work. Trimming and edging applies to the perimeter of your lawn, bed edges, and borders —anywhere grass creeps where it shouldn't. All you need are the right tools and knowledge on how to safely operate them to complete the job well.

The Dirt

While most of us use the terms *edging* and *trimming* interchangeably, they are entirely different practices. Edging is a vertical cut. Edgers usually have a metal blade that cuts into turf like a knife, creating a definitive line between turf on one side of the blade and the surface on the other side (pavement or mulch). Edging is performed monthly, just a few times each summer if your lawn is a cool-season grass.

Trimming is a horizontal cut achieved by a trimmer, most commonly a string trimmer. The head of a string trimmer resembles a hockey puck with two trimmer lines. The trimmer head spins at high speeds, and nylon line cuts through turf leaves. You will probably trim your lawn perimeter every time you mow.

EDGING WILL PREVENT creeping grass from overstepping its boundaries.

QUICK TIP

Trim edges so they are even to the height of your grass. A common mistake when using a string trimmer is to whip away too much length at property edges, creating a border that looks like a step down from the rest of the yard.

AN EDGER'S vertically turning head slices away turf.

Preliminaries

While dedicated equipment exists for trimming and edging, you'll probably want to purchase just one machine. Since trimming needs to happen more often, that is the most common choice. Gas-powered trimmers come in various sizes and styles. Their whipping action is ideal for cleaning up unruly turf around the perimeter of your home, and near trees, fences, or other places you can't access with a mower. Certainly, you can use a string trimmer to edge a lawn, turning the head so it trims vertically. Some trimmers are designed to operate effectively at this angle. But, don't expect the same clean-cut, definitive finish an edger will produce. You can purchase an edging attachment for some string trimmers, which is a versatile option.

An edging machine is engineered to deliver a vertical cut. A circular blade spins and slices into turf, swiftly cutting away scraggly grass that creeps into bordering areas like sidewalks or driveways. A stick edger is a more compact and less expensive version of this machine. It is also easier to store, if garage space is a concern. Stick edgers are close cousins to string trimmers, except they feature a blade attachment. You simply scoot the machine along the perimeter or desired edge, and the vibrating blade cuts neatly through turf. For a more hands-on approach, you can edge your lawn manually with a long-handled edging tool in the spade family or a wheel edger that you roll along the lawn perimeter. Both methods are effective and do not require power.

If you're serious about achieving perfect edges, invest in both a string trimmer and a stick edger.

Supplies
- **Eye protection**
- **Long pants**
- **String trimmer**
- **Stick edger or edging machine**

Always wear eye protection when operating power equipment. Hearing protection is also suggested when operating equipment that produces noise of 85 decibels or more, and most gas-powered lawn mowers and string trimmers exceed this level.

Steps

1. Trim or edge areas after mowing. That way, you can easily identify areas that need extra attention.

2. Using a string trimmer, trim grass around trees, near fences, around posts or utility boxes, and in other hard-to-reach places, such as under decks or around children's play equipment.

3. Switching to a stick edger, or turning your string trimmer in a vertical position, edge the perimeter of your lawn where grass meets walkways and driveways. Scoot the edging machine along the border slowly **(Figure 1)**.

Figure 1

PROJECT PAIRINGS

COMPLEMENT your neat-and-clean edges with these projects:

Tree & Shrub Pruning Clinic   36
Apply the same polished look to landscape elements.

Install Bed Edging   128
Enhance the border between landscape beds and your lawn.

PROJECT

Compost Technique

PREFABRICATED COMPOST
bins keep your pile contained.

Consider the waste generated by your landscape during a single year: grass clippings, deadheaded blossoms, leaves, and weeds. The byproducts of routine maintenance can pile up, but it also can be recycled into compost and incorporated into plant beds. Compost is nature's own soil amendment and mulch, and it is highly effective at increasing soil porosity, improving fertility, and stimulating healthy root development. Making your own is less expensive than buying garden center counterparts

The Dirt

Compost is the result of a variety of organisms breaking down plant materials. Organisms such as bacteria, fungi, worms, and insects live in the soil and love nothing better than a hearty meal of yard and kitchen wastes. Under the right conditions, these organisms efficiently convert compost materials into humus, a loamy, nutrient-rich soil. Humus is the end goal of composting, and it can take as long as a couple of years or as short as a month to produce it. We can speed up a process that may take Mother Nature a full season or years to achieve by establishing ideal conditions to promote decomposition.

Compost Variables

Air, water, temperature, and food dictate the speed at which compost material will break down. But first, what is your goal for composting? If you want materials to break down quickly so you can return them to your garden or plant beds a couple of times during the growing season, then you want to manage your compost. If you want the grass clippings to eventually break down, without a rush, then passive composting will work just fine.

The difference between managed and passive composting is speed, which requires your active participation. You can set up a compost pile or fill a bin and just wait. After a year or two the material will eventually compost. But if you want to force nature into the express lane, the managed compost technique steps in this project will explain how to hasten the process. You'll need a balance of carbon and nitrogen, the right temperature, good air circulation and the right amount of water. By mixing, chopping materials, and monitoring conditions in your compost pile, you'll increase your yield each season.

AIR

The best microbes for decomposing plant materials are aerobic, meaning they need oxygen. Without air, aerobic microbes die and their anaerobic cousins take over. Anaerobic microbes thrive without oxygen and decompose materials by putrefaction, which is smelly and slow. Anaerobic decomposition has an odor like rotting garbage. Aerobic decomposition smells musty and loamy, like wet leaves on the forest floor.

For the best air circulation, ensure that air passageways in your compost pile are not blocked. Combine heavier ingredients, such as grass clippings or wet leaves, with materials that allow air to penetrate, such as straw. Create layers of different textured materials, and turn the pile periodically to promote air circulation. Do this by using a garden fork or pitchfork to break apart the pile, and fluff it by restacking the pile.

WATER

A dry compost pile will delay the decomposition process, but a soaking wet pile chokes out necessary air circulation. Ideally, compost should be as wet as a wrung-out sponge. It should be coated, but not drenched, in water. That said, if you want to add dry leaves or straw to your compost pile, wet them with a hose as you add them in layers. But beware of too much wetness. Heavy, green grass clippings will need to dry out a bit to prevent weighing down your compost pile.

TEMPERATURE

When aerobic decomposition occurs, heat is produced. Tracking the temperature of your compost pile tells you how your pile is progressing. You can purchase compost thermometers at garden stores. Aim for a constant temperature between 104°F and 150°F (40°C to 54°C). At this temperature range, the pile is at its peak decomposition. Hotter piles decompose faster, but do not exceed temperatures above 160°F (71°C).

If your pile could use a warm-up, agitate the pile to increase air circulation and add nitrogen-dense materials like grass clippings or kitchen waste. Maintain a pile size of about 3 feet high and wide (1 cubic meter), which is enough mass to insulate the middle of the pile and prevent heat from escaping. Your compost is finished cooking when it looks like dirt and is no longer generating heat. Finally, rather than composting in piles, you can compost material in bins. Black, plastic-sided bins will maintain heat during the cooler weather.

Browns and Greens

Just as humans need a balance of nutrients for energy, so does a fast-burning compost pile. Compost consists of browns or greens. Browns are high in carbon, which is food energy that microorganisms depend on to decompose the pile. Greens are high in nitrogen, which is a protein source for the multiplying microbes. A ratio of 3 to 1 brown-to-green materials is the best balance.

Browns include dry brown plant material and straw. Dry brown weeds, wood chips, and saw dust can be used as browns with caution. Weed seeds are very difficult to kill unless the compost temperature is quite high. Wood chips from certain trees can be detrimental to compost organisms, and sawdust must be from unpainted and untreated wood. Greens include grass clippings, kitchen fruit and vegetable scraps, green leaves, and manure. If you treat your lawn with herbicides or pesticides, do not use clippings in the compost pile.

Preliminaries

The best time to start a compost pile in cool climate zones is in the spring, when warmer temperatures will jumpstart the decomposition process. Besides timing, pile placement is critical to the success (and speed) of composting. Choose a site that is well drained, and when building a pile rather than using a bin or container, make sure the plot is on soil and not your lawn or concrete. Soil houses all sorts of beneficial organisms, such as earthworms. They'll work to your benefit.

Also, pay attention to light exposure. Opt for a spot where you can take advantage of solar heat. If you live in a hot climate, choose an area in a shady portion of your property. That way, your pile won't lose moisture from evaporation. While you're selecting a site, consider starting the pile in a discreet area of your yard. Your plant bed should be a main landscape feature, not the pile of clippings you plan to eventually use as mulch.

Supplies
- **Garden fork or pitchfork**
- **Wheelbarrow**
- **Shovel**
- **Hose**
- **Green and brown material**

GREENS (1) AND BROWNS (2) are layered and mixed with a small amount of soil. Mix layers regularly by flipping and fluffing the pile with a garden fork or pitchfork.

If you compost kitchen waste, you can collect it in a convenient compost pail. Always keep a lid on the pail, unless you want to invite insects into your home. When you add scraps to the pile, cover them with about 8 inches (20.3 cm) of brown material. Do not add meat products or cheese to your compost pile. They don't decompose quickly, and their smell will attract critters.

Steps

1. Locate a site ideal for a compost pile (or bin) based on advice in Preliminaries.

2. Chop or shred compost materials. Doing so will speed up the decomposition process. Also, if you add materials such as grass clippings, be sure to dry them out slightly before adding to the pile so it can breathe. Same goes for leaves and kitchen waste.

3. Mix compost with a garden fork or pitch-fork. Combine one part of green material with three parts of brown material. Add a small amount of garden soil.

4. Build a pile at least 3 feet tall and wide (1 cubic meter).

5. As you build the pile, use a garden hose to lightly water layers that are particularly dry (usually this applies to brown material). Be careful not to overwater!

6. Turn or fluff up the compost mixture with a garden fork or shovel. Do this weekly. Consistent air circulation and churning will promote microbial breakdown.

7. Water the pile as necessary. Remember the wrung-out sponge comparison. Damp, but not wet, is your goal.

8. Compost is finished when the pile is wet, dark, crumbly, and smells like garden soil. Sift out larger pieces that did not decompose. Then, keep adding layers to your pile, continuing the process of chopping material, then layering, watering and turning it.

PROJECT PAIRINGS

NOW THAT YOU'VE MASTERED the art of making nutritious soil material, incorporate compost into these projects:

PROJECT

Control Deer

Your landscape is a tempting, green buffet for hungry deer and rabbits. Deer are especially over-populated in fast-developing suburban communities, and their grazing habits can take a toll on your plants and shrubs. Trying to convince deer that your plant bed isn't tasty isn't an easy task. The good news: You can

The best offense against deer is to use a variety of deterrents. Install fencing and begin using repellents early in the season. You can choose wildlife-resistant plantings. Ask a university extension for suggestions appropriate for your region.

protect your property from wildlife damage with repellents, fencing, and home remedies. These controls will help you redirect deer to a different feeding area, hopefully far away from your yard.

Identifying Marks

You'll notice subtle signs various critters are visiting your property.

Deer: Twigs and stems show a rough, shredded surface because deer lack upper incisors; deer also strip bark and leave no teeth marks.

Rabbits: Neat, sharp 45-degree cuts

Rodents: Narrow teeth marks

Netting and Tubing

Place netting around seedlings and small trees. Tubes protect tree trunks and young branches, though not all tubing will prevent bucks from scarping their antlers against tree trunks. Also, you can purchase paper bud caps, which form a protective cylinder and can reduce damage.

Fencing

There are several types: electric; a conventional fence of woven wire and mesh barriers. Check on neighborhood and city zoning regulations first.

A sturdy wood or metal fence at least 8 feet (2.4 m) high will deter deer from intruding, and there are plenty of options available at stores. But before you invest, check city and neighborhood ordinances. Many suburban

areas do not allow fences this tall. Instead, you might try temporary netting, which will send a keep-off message.

If your deer problem is more severe, you might consider electrical fences. Deer actually respond well to safe correction. They learn that plants beyond the barrier are not for them. A single-wire fence will protect a planting area, and you can always add wires if the deer problem escalates. For double-wire fences, place wires at 15 and 30 inches (38.1 and 76.2 cm) from the ground. Space wires at 10 inch (25.4 cm) increments for triple-wire fences.

Repellents

Contact repellents are applied directly to plants, and their foul taste discourages foraging. Area repellents cover an entire portion of a landscape, controlling deer by emitting a bad smell. Or, try a homemade remedy. Mix a solution of 20 percent raw eggs and 80 percent water. This will last about 30 days and is weather resistant. Soap bars and human or animal hair will keep deer away from plants for a while. But with any of these repellents, as deer grow accustomed to the smell or taste, if they are hungry enough, a stinky repellent won't prevent them from noshing. You'll need to alternate your choice repellent.

 WHAT ABOUT RABBITS?

If you notice neat, sharp 45-degree angle cuts in stems and trunks, your culprit is a rabbit. These critters will dig under wire fences to munch on garden goodies. To block their burrowing, you'll need to bury the wire fence 8 to 12 inches (20.3 to 30.5 cm) underground. Protect a young plant with a cylinder made from hardware cloth. Repellent sprays are also available to keep rabbits from feeding on foliage.

PROJECT

Landscaping with Mulch

Mulch blankets bare ground in plant beds and covers bald spots where grass won't grow. Aesthetically speaking, mulch enhances the look of a landscape, but its benefits run deeper than its surface appeal.

Mulch protects plant and tree roots, prevents soil erosion, discourages weed growth, and helps the ground retain moisture. You can choose organic or synthetic mulches; timing and technique are crucial, regardless.

The Dirt

Do you want your mulch to work for you by feeding nutrients to plants and soil? Or is your main goal appearance? Synthetic mulches and stones are long-lasting and even colorful, if you opt for tinted material. And synthetic mulch is a dead ringer for wood bark. You'll gain the moisture protection, erosion prevention, and weed control benefits from synthetic mulches, and they'll never break down.

But decomposition is one of the plusses of organic mulches, which range from compost to wood chips. They enrich soil and serve as hearty amendments, boosting soil with missing nutrients such as nitrogen. The downside to some organics is appearance. And because nature isn't perfect, mulch materials like lawn clippings and leaves get matted down when spread too thickly and exposed to too much moisture. In this instance, mulch will actually choke out air and moisture from soil, therefore sabotaging your good intentions.

The bottom line: Application technique is critical for organic, synthetic, or stone mulches. The most common material is shredded wood bark.

Following are other options:

ORGANIC
- **Compost**
- **Lawn clippings**
- **Leaves**
- **Wood chips or shavings**
- **Bark**

SYNTHETIC AND STONE
- **Recycled rubber**
- **Stone or brick**
- **Landscape fabric**

MULCH DISCOURAGES WEED growth and protects soil, while completing the look of landscaped areas.

If you opt for rubber or stone mulch, first lay down strips of landscape fabric. This will prevent mulch from mixing with soil.

Preliminaries

Before you apply mulch, remove weeds from the area and water all plants. You want a clean palette on which to spread new material. Following are other considerations:

Timing: Spread mulch in mid- to late-spring, after the ground warms up. If you apply mulch too soon, the ground will take longer to warm up and your plants will suffer for it. Depending on the time of year, you may need to lay down additional mulch to maintain soil health. Apply an extra layer of mulch in the summer to retain water, and in the winter to insulate soil. As temperatures warm in the spring, gradually lift away some mulch to allow new growth to sprout.

Density: Mulch that is too deep will prevent seedlings from sprouting and, in mature plants, promote root growth in the mulch layer. This is not what you want. The net result is a shallow root zone, which is especially detrimental under a thick layer of mulch that creates a blockade for water. Apply mulch with a light hand; you can always spread more later, if necessary.

Tricky Spots: Gravity, water, and wind can interfere with mulch performance. Consider heavier materials for slopes and areas exposed to high winds or flooding. Choose recycled rubber products that resemble traditional wood bark. These synthetic mulches will not break down with moisture, and they are less likely to blow around with wind or wash away with heavy rain.

Supplies

- **Wheelbarrow**
- **Shovel**
- **Mulch**
- **Garden rake**

Steps

1. Work in sections, scooping a pile of material from the load (in a wheelbarrow or a bag, depending on how you purchased it).

2. Gently spread mulch, ensuring even coverage of at least 1 inch (2.5 cm) to start.

3. Do not apply mulch within 1 or 2 inches (2.5 or 5.1 cm) of tree trunks and woody ornamentals. This will prevent insects and pests from attacking trees and shrubs **(Figure 1)**.

Figure 1

4. After spreading a thin layer, apply additional mulch if coverage is too thin to retain soil moisture. If you can see the ground, add more material.

5. You may choose to work organic mulch into the soil at the end of the season. It tends to gradually break down over the season, and by fall you can till it in with existing soil.

PROJECT PAIRINGS

NOW THAT YOUR BEDS are covered, try these projects:

PART THREE

Plants & Gardens

Pop goes the color! Delight in nature's confetti—a vibrant bed of annuals, or plumes of perennials peeking from containers and window boxes. In the garden, your imagination is your most valuable tool. Don't tame it. Rather, plant a garden that incorporates your favorites: colors, smells, textures, shapes. We'll provide the master plans if you're willing to get your hands dirty.

Color Clinic

Remember the color wheel from your elementary school art class? The rainbow pie is a snapshot of good, old Roy G. Biv. (That's red, orange, yellow, green, blue, indigo, violet for those of us with acronym-loving grade school teachers.) You remember mixing colors, learning which ones on the spectrum combine in harmony, and which muddle together in a muddy mess. Not exactly the effect you want for a garden space. Welcome back to the drawing board.

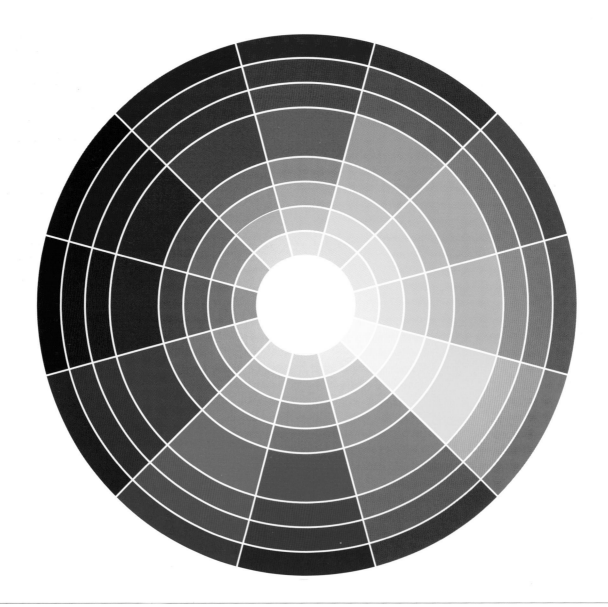

The color wheel is a valuable tool when choosing plant material for landscape beds. Not that your sense of style requires a tool, or a fix, but the inspiration a color wheel provides while picking plants makes the guide worth revisiting. A color wheel shows related, complementary, and contrasting colors. By understanding color relationships, you can plant a flower bed with colors that agree with one another.

Favorite Flavors

Color is rich in psychology. Consider what you already know about color and emotional triggers. Purple is royal, while red is passionate, and orange is creative. Yellow is happy, and green is healthy and growing. Red roses? Must be love.

Most of the time, we do not recognize how color affects our mood, we only know when we find visual pleasure in the hue. You may like pink for its charm, elegance, and soft playfulness. But probably, you'll simply choose pink flowering plants because the color appeals to you. And, it is perfectly fine to plan a flower bed by starting with the color you adore. In fact, this is a great place to start. A garden center manager confided that people are attracted to flower colors more than a plant's hardiness or price. We look for eye candy. So go ahead and indulge! Extensive choice in varietals will almost guarantee that you'll find an appropriate plant for your light and soil requirements.

The color play begins when you enhance this favorite color with background colors, fusing complementary hues into your landscape and accenting permanent fixtures such as stonework, your home, or patio furniture. Now, it is important to understand how colors work together and against each other.

For the most part, there are no distinct rules. But you probably fall into one of two camps: color, color everywhere; or less is more, keep it simple. Color fanatics look at the nursery like it's a candy store ready to be robbed and want one of everything. Subtle gardeners prefer a monoculture effect, meaning a range of flower varieties that are different shades of the same color. The result is actually quite powerful.

Choose Harmony

When choosing plants, it's helpful to understand which shades are neutral, and what complementary, related, and contrast colors mean. This project is your color tutorial. Your homework is to consider these color pairing principles while choosing plants, then throw out the rules if you decide to experiment. The color wheel and its lessons are guidelines, not bylaws.

Neutral: Whites, silvers, and greens are neutrals, and they serve as versatile backdrops for any color. You can lighten up bold reds, use them as transition plants to help different colors flow from one to the next, or simply plant all neutrals for a peaceful effect.

Related: These colors are located adjacent to one another on the color wheel. Choosing plants and flowers that are related in color will produce a uniform, soothing feeling. A landscape bed that contains varieties in shades of blue and purple exemplifies related colors in bloom.

Complementary: These colors fall across from one another on the color wheel. These pairs enhance one another, and this color combination method is ideal for livening up a landscape and creating drama. Yellow and purple are complementary because the sunny color brightens royal purple, which can look richer and take on an entirely different personality than when paired with blue or fuchsia.

Contrasting: These have three colors in between them on the color wheel. While they can add surprise to a landscape, a cohesive look can be difficult to pull off if you don't consider yourself color savvy. Because there are so many options in color and plant material, choosing appealing contrast colors takes more effort. It's not as simple as choosing a palette of pinks, which will naturally flow. Do try to mix purple and red, and experiment because when planting annuals, they'll only last one season. But if you are less of a plant lab rat, stick with related and complementary colors.

Layer Plant Beds

Layering holds multiple meanings in landscape design. There are layers of interest achieved by mixing various foliage textures, flower colors, and smells. Plant beds also contain layers of size: small, medium, and large varieties subtly arranged to draw the eye from the ground up. Then there are layers of blooming, which is a timing game. The goal, of course, is to maintain a constant show of color by planting varieties that peak during different seasons. In wintertime, color may come from berries or interesting foliage.

Therefore, creating a landscape bed involves design principles such as proportion, and science in understanding plant culture. We'll talk about these concepts in this project. They'll help you maximize your planting space and make a big impact.

The Dirt

The cardinal rule of gardening is to put the right plant in the right place. With this mantra always in mind, begin a landscape bed by imagining it as a blank canvas. What size is the space? Is the landscape bed close to a window or your deck, or is it farther away? Is there a theme you want to establish? Also important, what is your plant budget? If you are starting from scratch and your gardening piggy bank isn't fat, you'll want to begin small with a modest-sized bed. And as for location of the bed, if it serves as the border between your property line and the neighbor behind you, the plants you choose should be larger in scale.

NOTICE HOW THIS BED INCLUDES a variety of colors and textures, steps of plants that increase in size from small to large and appropriate proportion to the surroundings.

As you consider those questions and jot down notes, take into account the size and shape of your landscape bed. Is it accessible from one side or two? How wide is it? Is there a fence behind the bed that will support vine growth? Does the bed get full sun or mostly shade? Next, get personal. What colors do you prefer, and how would you describe your style? Formal landscape beds include neat shrubs and linear planting patterns, while wild perennial beds may incorporate wispy ornamental grasses and an array of native plants.

Use the above questions to create your plant palette.

Divide and Design

If your landscape bed is sizeable, divide it into workable sections before you choose plant material. For example, if the length of the space is 70 feet (21.3 m), break this area into three parts. This is a great way to establish repetition and consistency in your plantings. Treat each section as an entity and consider plant height, blooming period, and color.

Height: Each bed section should contain small, medium, and large plants, increasing in size from the front to back of the bed. If your bed is accessible from two sides, plant "anchor" or large plants in the middle row. Then, place a row of medium-sized plants on either side, followed by smaller plants on the borders.

Blooming period: Achieve a season-long show of color by choosing plants that bloom at different times. Do your homework before purchasing seedlings and plant material. If you pick varieties that peak all at once, what will you have to look forward to the rest of the season?

A LAYERED BORDER BED

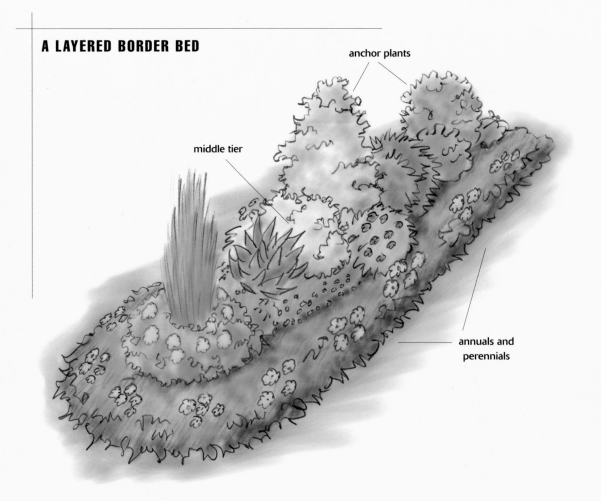

anchor plants

middle tier

annuals and perennials

Color: Refer to the Color Clinic on page 70 for advice on choosing related and complementary colors. But ultimately, select plant colors you favor, and don't forget to figure in the color of your pavers, home, patio furniture, and other permanent fixtures.

Thoughtful Placement

You'll need room to accomplish a layering effect. A 2-foot (0.6-m) wide bed strip just won't work, unless you only want a racing stripe of annuals. Beds should be at least 4 feet (1.2 m) wide to accommodate layering. If you can access the bed from both sides, you'll still be able to reach the center to care for the plants if the bed width is 6 feet (1.8 m).

When you choose plants, think about which ones retain their foliage all year. You should select some anchor plants that will serve as the backbone of your bed. You can always depend on them to offer interest. The middle layer of your bed can include selections that have some body, like flowering shrubs. You might choose a large hosta variety or lamb's ears, which are neutral and provide background for bright, flowering plants. Then, for the final layer, choose any variety of perennial flowers that bloom in spring, summer, or fall. Leave space between these plants to place annuals. That way, you always have a pop of color.

Proportion

How much space will your perennial flowering shrub consume in the bed after it matures? Be sure to allow enough room for growth. Planting isn't an instant gratification activity. If planted correctly, your bed will look young the first year, perhaps smaller in scale and not as high-impact as you planned. This is all right because it's necessary to leave space for plants to spread out.

If your bed looks too naked for your taste, annuals are the answer. Because they only last one season, you can plant them to fill space between young, developing perennials. Once perennials are mature, you still may want to add color during off-peak times. Also, because these plants last only one season, you can find what you like about different varieties.

Preliminaries

Remember the landscape plan from the first chapter? We discussed the importance of plotting out projects and getting ideas on paper. This exercise is also helpful for beds. Landscape architects rely on plans to map out where they will position plant material. It's a great way to experiment with different layouts before you dig in.

Supplies

- **Planting supplies** (page 31)
- **Plant material**

Steps

1. Start with a landscape bed plan as described in Preliminaries.

2. Prepare soil according to instructions in the Cottage Garden Master Plan project, page 76.

3. Begin planting in layers, starting at the back or middle of the bed with larger plants. Be sure to space plants according to growth information on plant tags. Do not cramp plants, otherwise you will have to move them once they are mature.

4. Include a mix of annuals, perennials, and foliage plants in your bed to achieve year-round color.

5. Water in plants, ensuring that soil is constantly moist the week after planting. Depending on the weather and climate where you live, you may water daily at first, tapering off after the first week plants take root.

PROJECT PAIRINGS

NOW THAT YOUR LANDSCAPE BED is alive with color year-round, consider these projects:

Attract Butterflies   90
Choose plants that lure in beautiful creatures.

Garden Benches   140
Enjoy a view of your hard work from a garden bench for two.

PROJECT

Cottage Garden Master Plan

Explore the wild side of planting with a cottage garden. These free-spirited gardens bloom with surprises—various colors, textures, and scents. Fragrant roses are hallmark cottage style, as is foliage that billows over pathways, and a quaint gate and arbor to show visitors where they can enter the whimsical space. A path leads the way through the mix of plants and landscape features. Cottage gardens are ideal spaces for antique accents, bird baths, and benches.

If your backyard is an escape from the daily grind, you'll appreciate the freedom and variety that cottage gardens introduce. Forget achieving a manicured look. Casual is okay in a cottage garden. In fact, these gardens are ideal learning gardens for beginners who want to improvise and play with plant possibilities.

But, there are a few ground rules to consider as you explore the beauty of random. A typical cottage garden contains these six features, in some form or another, rooms, living walls, fences, arbors, gates, and pathways.

Our project clinics cover these bases, and here we'll show you how to pull it all together, cottage style. Consider this your master plan.

The Dirt

Think of your cottage garden as a building—every structure needs a foundation. That would be the soil. As with any planting project, your first step is to prepare the bed. Fall is the best time for bed preparation, but any time you decide to tackle the task is fine. If you begin in early spring, make sure the soil is dry enough to work without clumping.

If you're starting from scratch with a cottage garden, your first step is to remove the turf and till the soil. You can remove turf by making horizontal cuts with a sharp spade about 2 inches (5.1 cm) down from the surface—but this is hard work. It is easier to rent either a manual or powered sod cutter. The manual version, often called a sod kicker, has a blade

that cuts through the sod roots as you push it across the turf. Use the cut turf to patch dead areas in your lawn, or allow it to dry thoroughly and add to your compost pile.

Tilling a garden for the first time can be tough going. Fortunately, you only have to do it once. You can do it by hand with a spade or garden fork or rent a tiller. Till the soil 8 to 10 inches (20.3 to 25.4 cm) deep. If you are working by hand, dig out a spade or a fork full, flip it upside down, and break up the clumps by hitting them with the edge of the tool. Take the time to remove weed roots and rocks and don't walk over the ground you just tilled, if at all possible.

Once you have turned over the garden bed, add soil amendments to provide a healthy home for your plantings. Repeat the tilling process to mix the amendments into the bed. Your planting area should contain equal parts peat moss, sand, and soil. If you're working with clay soil, you may improve the soil composition by adding more sand to improve porosity and water drainage. If soil is sandy, you'll want to add more peat moss and soil so your planting area will retain water and nutrients. Balance is the key.

Preliminaries

Because cottage gardens do call for certain key elements, you'll want to map out a design so you can decide which features to include. Your arbor and gate form an entrance—the welcome sign to your cottage garden, in a sense. From there, a pathway will lead visitors through the garden rooms or planting areas. You can differentiate these rooms by choosing different feature plants, adding a focal point

 **DESIGN TIP**

Cottage gardening indeed has a few standard procedures, but flexibility makes this style easy. Add accessories like statues, bird baths, benches, fountains, or antiques.

 PLANT PICKS

- **Foxglove**, *Digitalis purpurea*—Flowers form on a spike, ranging in color from deep purple to lilac; leaves form a rosette the first year followed by a flower spike the next near.
- **Coreopsis**, *Coreopsis tinctoria*—Yellow, daisy-like flowers can be deep gold in color; a relative of the sunflower.
- **Hydrangea**, *Hydrangea*—Tender shrubs boast large flowers; find them in white, pink, red and blue.
- **Viburnum**, *Viburnum*—Versatile shrubs feature showy, fragrant flowers and colorful berries and foliage in fall.
- **Lamb's ears**, *Stachys byzantina*—Known for silvery foliage, light-purple flowers bloom on spikes; spreads quickly.
- **Purple coneflower**, *Echinacea purpurea*—Otherwise known as *Echinacea*, their broad petals provide nice resting spots for butterflies.
- **Balloon flower**, *Platycodon*—Blue-blooming and easy to grow; buds look like hollow balloons, which gradually inflate and deepen in color.
- **Daylily**, *Hemerocallis*—Available in a variety of colors, daylilies grow almost anywhere.
- **Larkspur**, *Delphinium*—Deep, blue-purple flowers grow on spikes.
- **English roses**—Often called David Austin roses; known for their fragrant cupped or rosette-shaped petals.

like a statue, or incorporating a bench where visitors can admire the environment.

After creating your plan, devise a plant list with the help of a professional at your local nursery or garden center. Explain your goals, and be sure to include feature, filler, and anchor plants. These plants are your living walls, which divide your rooms. See how it all comes together?

The most important preliminary to note with this project is that yes, there are some rules to cottage gardening. But who says your garden isn't whimsical or beautiful if you decide to only incorporate a couple cottage-style features? There are countless adaptations you can make as you accomplish this project. And you may choose to complete this project in phases over a period of several years. Perhaps you decide to start with Step One and choose layers of plants. Or, perhaps you lay a pathway and begin working on one room at a time. Let the five principles of cottage garden *guide* you, but not restrict you.

Supplies
- **Planting supplies** (page 31)
- **Pathway** (See project on page 124.)
- **Arbor** (See project on page 134.)
- **Gate** (See project on page 194.)
- **Plants that serve as "living walls"** such as Wegiela, boxwood, evergreen or conifers

Steps (See opposite page.)

1. Choose feature, filler, and anchor plants. Feature plants are the main event. English roses are classic cottage style. Filler plants may include hydrangeas, and viburnum provides depth. Anchor plants stand tall in the background: evergreens, conifers, boxwoods and other small trees. Annuals can serve as borders and define the lines in your garden. *(See Plant Picks on page 78 for more suggestions.)*

2. Create rooms. Rooms are areas you define so the garden can be viewed in segments. You don't want to view the whole thing at once; you may miss a detail or get lost in the variety infused in cottage gardens. Room size is relative to the size of garden you establish. Most people work with a space on a typical subdivi-sion lot, so garden rooms may range from 8 by 10 feet (2.4 by 3 meters) to 11 by 14 feet (3.4 by 4.3 meters).

3. Grow living walls. To separate rooms, you need walls—living dividers that grow 6 to 8 feet (1.8 to 2.4 meters) tall. Wegiela, a blooming plant, or boxwood hedging are practical choices. Evergreen and conifers also work well to establish distinctive frames in a cottage garden.

4. Fence it in. A fence defines your property and establishes a private space for your cottage garden. Fences are not to keep everyone out, but instead to protect your secret space.

5. Add an Arbor. An arbor arching above emphasizes the feeling of entering a space.

6. Get a gate. Gates are powerful symbols, but they need not conform to traditional whitewashed wood. Gates can be plain, unpainted wood, iron, painted bright purple—use your imagination.

7. Plant pathways. Curved, angular, brick or stone—pathways draw lines and provide a traffic pattern for visitors. Those lines are blurred when you allow foliage and flowers to creep on to stepping stones. These soft lines are characteristic of cottage gardens.

PROJECT PAIRINGS

CREATE FEATURES for your cottage garden with these projects:

PROJECT

Drought-Tolerant Landscapes

Lush, green grass is the all-American standard, and a landscape expectation we mistakenly pursue in regions where hot, dry conditions will inevitably botch plans for a perfect emerald lawn. Grass is what front yards are made of, right? Grass is to a yard as siding is to a house. Well, not always.

The reality is not every environment provides ideal soil, rainfall, or temperatures to accommodate turf and other thirsty plants. Enter xeriscape, a term coined by the Denver, Colorado Water Department in 1981 in response to drought conditions. Now, the term is widely used to describe a drought-tolerant method of landscaping designed to conserve water.

Xeriscape is a holistic approach to landscape design, plant selection, irrigation, and maintenance. Forget ideas that xeriscape is nothing but dirt lawns and rock gardens. You can achieve a colorful, texturally interesting landscape by incorporating plants, ornamental grasses, and turf that thrive in climates with low precipitation. In this project, we'll provide a rough landscape plan modeled on the key principals of xeriscaping. Adapt it to fit your property's conditions.

The Dirt

Xeriscape addresses issues concerning irrigation, plant selection, and maintenance by developing a strategy many desert communities and scant precipitation regions adopt today. The seven basic principles of xeriscaping include: water-wise planning and design; low water use and drought-tolerant plants; limited lawn areas; efficient irrigation design and equipment; water harvesting techniques; surface mulches and soil amendments; and proper maintenance practices.

Zone in on Design

In designing a landscape modeled after xeriscape principals, you'll divide your property into zones based on water availability. The oasis zone, closest to your home, is the best place to plant turf, annuals, potted plants or to lay a paver patio, which will direct roof-water runoff to nearby plant beds. High water-use plants help cool the home. The next layer out from the home is the transition zone. By utilizing water harvesting techniques, such as channeling runoff, directing water to the area via sloping terraces, and collecting roof water, you can provide necessary moisture to drought-tolerant trees, shrubs and groundcovers. Finally, the arid zone includes plants that can survive on rainwater, likely the property's natural vegetation.

Choose Hardy Plants

Whether your backyard is a desert or you are experiencing a particularly dry season, select "survivor" plants that ease the burden on your water table and look great without steady rainfall. When choosing plant material, tune in to soil requirements listed on tags. Look for clues like "sandy" or "well drained." Plants that require rich, fertile soil will need amendments, humus, water, and lots of care in drought environments. Remember, the object of xeriscape is to reduce maintenance and conserve water. So opt for succulents, ornamental grasses, wildflowers, native plants (refer to a university extension for suggestions), and rock garden plantings. (See Rock Garden on page 114.)

Preliminaries

Before you begin this project, map out your property and note areas that collect rainfall. Do you notice that turfgrass does not thrive in a certain area? Could you install hardscape, such as a patio space, which would promote water run-off into nearby planting beds? Do you rely solely on an irrigation system for watering; how frequently does it rain? From there, determine the oasis, transition, and arid zones of your property. Now, you're ready to plant and landscape the xeriscape way.

Supplies

Refer to these projects for instructions and supplies for portions of this xeriscape design project:

- **Planting supplies,** page 31
- **Drip Irrigation,** page 48
- **Landscaping with Mulch,** page 66

Buffalo Grass

St. Augustine Grass

Zoysia Grass

Kentucky Bluegrass

You don't have to eliminate turf from your landscape plan. Just minimize your grassy plot and be sure it's located in an "oasis" area close to the home where moisture is more readily available. Depending on your region, choose varieties such as buffalo grass, St. Augustine grass, zoysia grass, or Kentucky Bluegrass.

Steps

1. Choose drought-tolerant plants. Refer to The Dirt for plant selection details. Add textural interest with ornamental grasses. Succulents like cacti are available in flowering species that add a pop of color to a landscape. Opt for groundcovers like sedum, which is popular for rock gardens and also available in flowering varieties. Plant native flowers, such as purple coneflower (*echinacea*) and wildflowers. Refer to Layering Plant Beds on page 72 for planting tips.

2. Limit lawn areas. If you choose turfgrass, opt for a drought-tolerant variety and plant it near access to water run-off.

3. Install drip irrigation. Refer to the Drip Irrigation project on page 48 for instructions. This economical method of watering plant beds is ideal for drought-prone regions. An alternative is to use a low-volume spray or misting hose, which will provide just enough water to satisfy plants without causing run-off.

4. Harvest water. You can collect, or harvest, water by channeling runoff to planted areas or containing it for later use. Collect rainwater from your roof or direct it into a plant bed basin. Shallow basins dug around plant beds create a similar effect to irrigation basins that farmers use to feed crops. Water collects in basins and penetrates soil in the bed area. Another tactic is to install a hardscape patio or sloping terraces. Rainwater glides off the surface, traveling farther out to the property to reach plants or turf.

5. Mulch and amendments. By laying mulch or soil amendments on plant beds, you can trap moisture and maintain cooler soil temperatures, therefore conserving water.

6. Lawn care best practices. Do not overfertilize your lawn; this promotes rapid growth (and higher demand for water). Heavy pruning has the same effect: shrubs and trees branch out and get thirsty. Do not cut your lawn too short, otherwise you will promote shallow root growth, and shallow roots look for water close to the surface level. Deep roots take longer to dry out and thrive better in drought environments. Finally, water on an as-needed basis, using drip irrigation and similar water conversation techniques.

PROJECT PAIRINGS

THESE LANDSCAPE PROJECTS are ideal for drought-prone properties:

Install Drip Irrigation 48
Conserve water by installing a delivery system that won't cause run-off.

Rock Garden 114
Add textural interest and color with a well-designed outcropping.

Zen Space 118
This meditative landscape style is also kind to the water table.

Ground Cover

Ground cover is a living canvas. It provides texture and interest to a landscape, fills patches where turf refuses to grow, and serves as an attractive transition between planting areas. What's more, a carpet of vegetation will work as a soil advocate. Ground cover prevents erosion and protects soil from harsh elements.

Ground cover refers to any vegetation that provides a dense, even cover. Though you might associate ground cover with a creeping ivy or low-growing pachysandra, it includes evergreen and deciduous plants, herbaceous and woody species, ornamental grasses, perennials, and annuals. For example, carpet roses spread similarly to common ivy, but their fragrant and colorful buds

wallpaper soil with a beautiful reward. A nursery professional can advise you on appropriate choices for your soil type and climate.

Here we'll show you how to prepare soil and plant tempting ground cover. You'll notice how this process is really no different from installing perennials in a bed.

The Dirt

If cared for properly, ground cover will: stabilize soil; grow in areas where turf will not; and provide texture, color, and interest. Ground cover is an ideal for controlling erosion, and also a great help to soil, in general. Because it serves as a protective layer, it can restore moisture and prevent compaction.

Because many ground covers are of a spreading nature, it is important to think of containment before planting. It can be hard to imagine that a few little seedlings will someday take over your yard, but it has happened to many a gardener. Use edging at least 4 inches (10.2 cm) deep to contain creeping and spreading.

Common Covers

Climate, along with light and water requirements, dictates what type of ground cover will thrive in your yard. But here is a list of common varieties:

- **Creeping Juniper**—full sun
- **English Ivy**—partial shade
- **Lantana**—full sun
- **Lily of the Valley**—shade
- **Myrtle**—partial shade
- **Pachysandra**—partial to full shade
- **Sedum**—full sun (drought-tolerant)

Avoid planting ground cover in mid-summer, when hot sun adds stress to young ground cover plants. Take on this project in fall or early spring. That way, root systems will develop before the hot, dry months.

Preliminaries

Investigate the planting area, noting sun exposure. Are there trees or structures that create shady spots in the area to be planted? Adhere to the master gardener's rule, and put the right plant in the right place.

Prepare soil before planting. Loosen soil, working it to a depth of 8 to 10 inches (20.3 to 25.4 cm). Incorporate a layer of organic matter, such as peat moss or compost. For compacted soil, you may want to add sand to improve its porosity. If planting around a tree, you may be limited by roots. In this case, plant where you can. As the plant matures it will fill in around the roots.

Finally, be sure that plants you purchase are healthy. Soil dries out quickly in flats no deeper than ice cube trays. If soil is dry in the store, plants are stressed and roots systems may not recover from the neglect.

Supplies
- **Planting supplies** (page 39)
- **Plant material**
- **Water**

Steps

1. Prepare soil as indicated in Preliminaries. Then smooth the planting area with a rake until level, being careful not to compact the surface.

2. Lay out plants in a staggered grid pattern. Refer to the plant stake for planting distances. Placing plants too closely will cause roots to compete for water and nutrients. While the area may look spare in early growth stages, the ground cover will fill in and mature within about two years.

3. Lift each plant from its spot and, using a trowel or your fingertips, dig a hole in the soil.

4. Remove the plant from the pot and set it in the hole, and gently press down roots so they make contact with soil. Repeat this process for each plant.

5. Water in plants, ensuring that soil is constantly moist the first week after planting. But be careful not to overwater. You should not allow standing pools of water to form at the base of plants. After plants begin to take root, you can ease off your daily watering schedule. Spread a thin layer of mulch around young ground cover plants to prevent soil from losing moisture and protect against erosion.

PROJECT PAIRINGS

NOW THAT YOU'VE GOT your ground covered, try these complementary projects:

Container Planting Clinic   104
Ground cover is a textured backdrop for a collection of potted plants.

Install Bed Edging   128
Contain ground cover with functional, decorative borders.

Build an Arbor   138
Ground cover is the feature presentation when you appoint the area with a formal entrance.

PROJECT

Vines for Landscapes

Vines are like wallpaper, in a sense. They cloak brick and stone surfaces in green; they shinny up and over fences. Vines cling to trellises and curl around topiary forms, and they can be trained to grow just about anywhere. In a courtyard setting, the green climbers lend an English garden feel, acting as rich, textured background, a perfect stage for delicate roses. Their vertical growing habit makes wise use of space if your property is the size of a thumbprint.

But be careful. The same spreading characteristic that is beneficial in ground cover applications is a curse for gardeners who naively plant vines without an understanding of their invasiveness. Certain cultivars can escape from a garden space and take over surrounding areas. In fact, entire forests have been invaded by runaway ivy planted by unassuming gardeners. Invasive ivy is like a rash that spreads—if you choose the wrong variety. (*See Noninvasive Ivies on page 89.*)

If you've already built an arbor, created a cottage garden, or constructed a trellis (all projects contained in this book), vines are a complementary embellishment you can grow easily. Vines also do a great job of hiding undesirables in your yard, which we'll discuss further in Operation Conceal, page 190.

The Dirt

Perennial vines are versatile, hardy, and available in varieties that flower, have colored foliage such as red, or feature interesting-shaped leaves. Vines are usually woody or semiwoody climbing or trailing plants, but some vines have herbaceous stems that die back each winter. Each species and cultivar has distinct characteristics.

Annual vines must be seeded annually. Some are noted for their continuous blooms, while others have distinctive foliage. The benefit of an annual vine is that

if you don't like a vine in that location, it will be gone the following year.

You probably associate vines with common English ivy, growing up a wall. But just as there are many varieties of vines, there are many ways to display them.

The following are ideal ways to grow vines:
- **Draping** from hanging baskets
- **Spilling** from containers set in gardens
- **Cascading** from window boxes on balconies or from windows
- **Spreading** over arbors and pergolas
- **Clambering** over a chain-link fence or covering an eyesore
- **Twining** up or around a tree
- **Covering** a trellis
- **Climbing** a wall

WAY TO GROW

Growth Habits

Take care to study vines and the multitude of varieties available before selecting a type for your project. They grow and climb in different ways; some cling and others do not. Some are deciduous and produce fragrant flowers, others are evergreens. For example, clematis is available in evergreen and deciduous cultivars, and ranges in color from pink to blue. So do your homework, and consider your climate. Which vine varieties will thrive? A professional at a garden center will help you find an appropriate option. You should also read up on vines before you allow them to get attached in your landscape. (See Resources at the back of this book for suggestions.)

Vines are classified by the way they grow. Vines are either climbing or nonclimbing. Nonclimbing vines grow long stems like vines but have difficulty growing vertically without a support. Rambling rose falls into this category. Climbing vines have a number of methods for attaching themselves to vertical structures or surfaces. These climbing methods are:

Twining: The stems of these vines wrap around a vertical support. Popular wisteria and bittersweet are twining vines **(A)**.

Tendrils: These vines have tendrils that reach out from the stem to wrap around any type of support. Grapes are a common vine with tendrils **(B)**.

Clinging: Clinging vines attach to flat surfaces with adhesive disks like Virginia creeper or small aerial rootlets like English Ivy **(C)**.

Preliminaries

This project outlines how to start vines outdoors. For instructions on pruning and care, refer to the Ivy Topiary project on page 112, or Tree & Shrub Pruning Clinic on page 36. The former provides advice on training ivy and other vine plants; the clinic offers information on pruning best practices. You'll purchase vines in containers from a garden center, so follow the planting rules in Ground Cover, page 84. Notes in the project for preparing the bed, spacing plants, and watering all apply.

HEALTHY CHOICES

Perennial Vine Varieties

HERE ARE SOME VINES you will discover as you explore the world of climbing plants—and it is a vast one. Always refer to the USDA Plant Hardiness Zone Map on page 215 when choosing material, and determine light exposure and soil quality in the spot you plan to grow your vines. Choose the right vine for your climate and property.

English ivy, *Hedera helix* (various)
Boston ivy, *Parthenocissus tricuspidata*
Wisteria, *Wisteria* (various)
Clematis, *Clematis microphylla*
Climbing Hydrangea, *Hydrangea petiolaris* (various)
Rambling roses, *Rosa* (various)

NonInvasive Ivies

THE AMERICAN IVY SOCIETY selects an Ivy of the Year annually, and each cultivar is easy to grow, hardy, lush, beautiful, and not invasive in the garden—a critical point we make earlier in this project. Try growing one of these suggested ivies:

Lady Frances, *Hedera helix*
Teardrop, *Hedera helix*
Golden Ingot, *Hedera helix*
Duck Foot, *Hedera helix*
Misty, *Hedera helix*
Anita, *Hedera helix*
Shamrock, *Hedera helix*

For more information on non-invasive ivies, visit www.ivy.org.

Now, let's get started! Vines are versatile and easy to grow. They are relatively drought-tolerant and adapt to sunny and shady spaces, though you should be sure the variety you select does not have special light requirements. Vines are quick to latch on to the support you design for them, but choose a strong skeleton if you plan to grow a woody stemmed vine. Permanent structures such as fences, pergolas, and trellises fit the bill. But do not grow vines on a wood-sided home. Vines will trap moisture and encourage rotting of the siding.

Supplies

- **Trellis, wall, or fence**
- **Planting supplies** (page 31)

Steps

1. Choose a support for your vine. Note the planting location, its light exposure and soil. Choose a vine variety according to the preferred growth habit.

2. Purchase potted vine plants at a garden center. Transplant plants to desired location, according to instructions in Ground Cover, page 84.

3. During the first growing season, tie vines to the trellis with string or netting to encourage growth on the support. Prune after the first bloom to stimulate branching (for blooming varieties). If the vine is stubborn to form leaves on the lower portion of the stem, promote horizontal growth before directing the vine upward. Do this by tying existing stems horizontally on your support until shoots form on the bare portion of the vine. Then, revert to vertical training.

PROJECT PAIRINGS

Need to build a support for your vine? These projects will show you how:

Ivy Topiary 112
Prim and proper topiaries involve training ivy to form a classic two-tiered design.

Build an Arbor 134
Vines will dress up this quintessential gateway to the cottage garden.

Operation Conceal 190
Create a support you can lean against a surface or build into a pergola.

PROJECT

Attract Butterflies

Butterflies are nature's ballet company.
The delicate creatures flutter about, dance in sunlight, which they love, and pose gracefully on petal tips, sipping sweet drinks of their favorite elixir: nectar. You can encourage butterflies to visit your garden by planting flowers rich in this substance. We'll show you how to create a habitat so you can lure in butterflies and persuade them to stay in your yard so you can enjoy the show.

The Dirt

To attract a continuous succession of butterflies, plant a combination of nectar-producing plants with overlapping blooming periods. That way, your landscape always contains flowers at their peak. Annuals are always enticing because they bloom continuously throughout the summer season, when butterflies are most active. Perennial plants with wide blooms like coneflowers give butterflies a place to safely land and comfortably perch while they enjoy nectar. Perennials with bunches of small blooms are also appealing.

Also, a range of plant sizes will attract a spectrum of butterflies. Small butterflies tend to hover closer to the ground, while large butterflies with generous wingspans soar high toward flowering trees or fruit-bearing bushes. Favored flowering trees also provide a place for butterflies to seek shade and shelter from wind and cold. Try planting a Red Bird of Paradise or Chaste Tree.

The most effective butterfly gardens provide food for adult butterflies and caterpillars. You want to appeal to butterflies at every stage of life. This process begins when a caterpillar hatches out of its egg, eats this egg, and then munches on a host plant. Popular host plants include milkweed, aster, cherry and blueberry bushes. Next, the caterpillar molts several times before changing into a pupa and, finally, emerges as an adult butterfly.

The key is to plant options—a nectar buffet.

Preliminaries

There's more to attracting butterflies than planting sweet flowers. You must create a habitat with features that butterflies enjoy. Think of this project as your plan for a butterfly playground. Besides selecting the right plants, you'll also include:

- **Sunny** areas and open spaces
- **Shade** trees and shrubs for nesting and protection
- **Puddles**
- **A feeder**

This project serves as a roadmap to help you establish a habitat with a variety of features, including plants that butterflies find appealing. For specific information on how and when to plant, refer to previous projects.

Supplies

- **Planting supplies** (page 31)
- **16" (40.6 cm) diameter shallow planter saucer or tray**
- **Sand or gravel**
- **Plant material**
- **Small jar with lid**
- **Sugar**
- **Cotton ball**
- **Drill**
- **String**

Steps (See opposite page.)

1. Plant a variety: Select a range of annuals and perennials, along with shrubs and trees, that will attract butterflies. Plant different sizes and flowers with various blooms.

2. Sun spots: Butterflies love to bask in the sun. Be sure your property has open spaces that allow light exposure.

3. Shade areas: During cool or windy weather, butterflies like to hide in trees and bushes that protect them from the elements. They also prefer to nest in foliage plants.

 BUTTERFLY PLANT PICKS

REMEMBER, SELECT A VARIETY OF PLANTS that bloom at different times. You'll always give butterflies a reason to visit. Refer to your local university extension for specific plant suggestions for your region. Following is a general guide:

Aster, *Astrum*
Black-eyed Susan, *Thunbergia alata*
Butterfly weed, *Asclepias tuberosa*
Chaste Tree, *Vitex agnus-castus*
Coreopsis, *Coreopsis tinctoria*
Black Dalea, *Dalea frutescens*
Daylilies, *Hemerocallis*
Desert milkweed, *Asclepias subulata*
Dill, *Anethum graveolens*
Goldenrod, *Solidago odora*
Hibiscus, *Hibiscus moscheutos*
Lantana, *Lantana camara*
Lavender, *Lavandula*
Lilac, *Syringa vulgaris*

Marigold, *Calendula officinalis*
Nasturtium, *Tropaeolum majus*
Oxeye Daisies, *Leucanthemum vulgare*
Peony, *Paeonia*
Petunia, *Petunia x hybrida*
Blue phlox, *Phlox divaricata*
Pink Azalea, *Rhododendron periclymenoides*
Purple Coneflower, *Echinacea purpurea*
Queen Anne's Lace, *Daucus carota* (North America)
Anthriscus sylvestris (Europe)
Red Bird of Paradise, *Caesalpinia pulcherrima*
Redbud, *Cercis occidentalis*
Rosemary, *Rosmarinus*
Verbena, *Verbena*

AN ATTRACTIVE HABITAT

THIS LANDSCAPE PLAN includes features that will attract butterflies:

1. **Various sized plants with different blooming periods**
2. **Sunny spots**
3. **Shade areas**
4. **Puddles**
5. **A feeder**

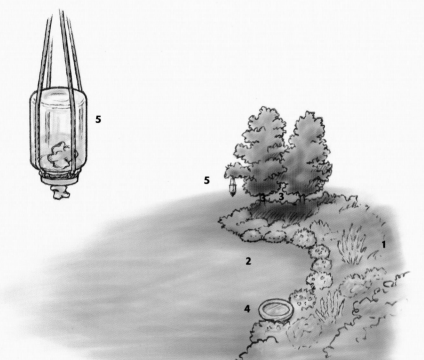

4. Make puddles: Rain puddles are a common gathering space for butterflies, and you can create your own garden puddle with a planter saucer. Simply bury it into the ground by digging a hole deep enough to hold the saucer without covering the brim. Fill the saucer with gravel or sand, and then pour in water, a sweet drink, or stale beer.

5. Add a feeder: Supplement flower nectar with a feeder made from a small jar. Drill a hole in the center of the lid, and plug this hole with a cotton ball. Fill the jar with 1 part sugar (not honey) to 9 parts warm water. Stir to mix until the sugar dissolves. Fasten the lid onto the jar. Attach bright, fabric petals to the lid to make it more appealing. Tie string around the jar and hang, lid downward, in a tree or bush.

PROJECT PAIRINGS

TRY THESE complementary projects:

Color Clinic   70
Plants that attract butterflies are available in a range of blooming colors. Consider these tips for choosing the right options for your garden.

Layering Plant Beds   72
Learn how to arrange plantings in a functional, aesthetically pleasing manner.

Cottage Garden Master Plan   76
Incorporate plants that attract butterflies into your cottage garden.

PROJECT

Herb Garden

Garden-fresh herbs are a satisfying and personal accompaniment to a home-cooked meal. From seed to soil, straight to the dinner table, the aroma of fresh herbs is more concentrated than their packaged, commercial counterparts, and their flavors are more complex. Besides, there is nothing better than gathering items on your grocery list from your own backyard. Planting an herb garden means having an array of gourmet flavors within view of your kitchen window.

You can plant a bounty of herbs to cook with by following the basic planting model in this project. We include a list with seventeen different herbs, but you can always omit selections or double the amount of your favorites. A dozen different herbs will provide variety and visual interest.

The Dirt

Herbs can be perennial, annual, and biennial (living for two seasons and blooming only the second season). Perennials overwinter and bloom each season. However, tender perennials like basil or lemon verbena are considered annuals in cold climates because they do not survive severe winters. You'll notice both on our Beginner's Herb Garden plant list on page 96.

Plants are classified as perennials and annuals depending on their zones. For example, say a plant tag says "Perennial in Zone 10," which means the coldest temperatures it will tolerate are 30 to 40 degrees Fahrenheit (−1 to 4 degrees Celsius). If you live in a cold climate, this plant is an annual because it will not withstand the winter. In a warm climate, no problem. So always double-check the hardiness zone when purchasing a perennial, because the herb may not tolerate your climate if it is not that exact zone. (See the USDA Plant Hardiness Zone Map in Resources, page 215.)

THE PECONIC RIVER HERB FARM in Calverton, N.Y., includes a collection of beginner's herbs. See the plan to learn how to make one in your yard.

Plant selections from this project are in **bold**.

Annuals: anise, **basil**, chervil, coriander, dill, summer savory, **rosemary**, **German chamomile**, **lemon verbena**

Biennials: parsley, caraway

Perennials: chives, **bee balm**, fennel, mint, **Mexican marigold mint**, **French tarragon**, **sweet marjoram**, **broadleaf English thyme**, **narrow leaf French thyme**, **silver edge thyme**, **golden lemon thyme**, **garden sage**, **pineapple sage**, **Greek oregano**

Planting a Seed

There are various types of herbs, but this project will focus on the ones you'll want to eat. Besides culinary herbs, there are medicinal herbs thought to have curative powers, and aromatic herbs that can be used to produce perfumes. Not sure where to start? Check your supermarket aisle.

Most herbs can be grown from seed or purchased at your local nursery. Some herbs such as mint and bee balm have a tendency to over-take a garden. It is best to plant these in a pot and sink them into the ground to confine their root systems. The best time to plant herbs is in the spring, after the last frost. (For more planting tips, see Ground Cover, page 84.)

Structural Integrity

A traditional herb garden features symmetrical paths to define the structure of the planting space and a central decorative feature. The garden you will create in this project is adorned with a bird bath, but you can improvise and include statuary, ornate planters, or even a water fountain.

Plant beds of individual herbs in geometric patterns, such as triangles with a diamond center; arches in corners and square beds in the center; or a circle-shaped bed with sections that look like pie slices. You'll notice that the herb garden shown below is arranged with blocks of herbs contained in a square garden. Landscape timbers act as borders, holding together the design.

BEGINNER'S HERB GARDEN

Plant list

1. **Basil,** *Ocimum basilicum*
2. **Broadleaf English thyme,** *Thymus vulgaris*
3. **Narrow-leaf French thyme,** *Thymus vulgaris* 'Narrow Leaf French'
4. **Garden sage,** *Salvia*
5. **Chives,** *Allium schoenoprasum*
6. **Silver-edge thyme,** *Thymus argentia*
7. **Golden lemon thyme,** *Thymus citriodorus*
8. **Greek oregano,** *Origanum heracleoticum*
9. **Sweet marjoram,** *Majorana hortensis*
10. **Rosemary (potted),** *Rosmarinus officinalis*
11. **German chamomile,** *Matricaria recutita*
12. **Parsley,** *Petroselinum crispum*
13. **Bee balm,** *Monarda didyma*
14. **Lemon verbena,** *Aloysia triphylla*
15. **Pineapple sage,** *Salvia elegans*
16. **Mexican marigold mint,** *Tagetes lucida*
17. **French tarragon,** *Artemisia dracunculus*
18. **Slate stepping stones**
19. **Bird bath**

You can grow herbs indoors year-round. They thrive in containers, but be careful where you place them. Select a south- or west-facing window, as most herbs require a sunny location. Perennials perform best outdoors during summer months, but bring them back indoors before the first frost.

Preliminaries

When choosing a site for your herb garden, consider drainage and soil fertility. Herbs will not grow in wet soils, nor do they prefer overly fertile environments. Therefore, you should use little, if any, fertilizer. If you must improve a site with poor drainage, you can modify the soil by removing 15 to 18 inches (38.1 to 45.7 cm) of it and placing a 3-inch (7.6-cm) layer of crushed stone or similar material. This improves soil porosity and allows for better drainage. Before returning soil to the bed area, mix it with compost (or sphagnum peat) and coarse sand. This will lighten the soil texture, also promoting water filtration. Refill the bed higher than the original level to allow for soil settling. A couple of inches (5.1 cm) will suffice. If your soil is healthy and drains well, simply churn up 6 to 12 inches (15.2 to 30.5 cm) of the soil using the forking method described in Cottage Gardens Master Plan page 76.

Supplies

- **Planting supplies** (page 31)
- **Plant material**
- **Landscape timbers or other border**
- **Bird bath or decorative ornament**
- **Stone pavers**

Steps

1. Map out your herb garden by drawing a sketch. Outline the shape of the bed, and determine the geometric shapes you will form with plantings. Use this as an outline when you plant, or use the one shown on page 96.

2. Define your bed by creating a border.

3. Prepare soil according to instructions in Preliminaries.

4. Place your central decorative feature first and use this as a guideline, planting around it.

5. Plant and water herbs according to your sketch. Refer to Ground Cover, page 84, for planting tips.

6. Add optional finishing touches, such as pavers.

PROJECT PAIRINGS

YOU'LL LIKELY TAKE ON more cooking projects in the kitchen as you experiment with your homegrown herbs. But before you head indoors, try these complementary projects:

Garden Benches   140

Build a place to sit in your herb garden, and enjoy the sweet and pungent aromas of your plantings.

Maximize a Small Space   206

Compact yards are ideal plots for herb gardens. You don't need much room to grow a bounty.

PROJECT

Hypertufa Planter

Searching for nostalgia in all the wrong places? Rather than sourcing sought-after antique stone or concrete trough-style planters, and paying more than you'd like for such weathered treasures, make your own hypertufa reproduction.

The word *hypertufa* is derived from *tufa*, a light porous rock. Hypertufa is a lightweight, functional material and isn't nearly as heavy as stone or concrete planters, so you can create forms to mold versatile hypertufa into any shape you desire. In this project, we'll show you how to create a convincing knockoff of an aged stone trough.

The Dirt

The appropriate hypertufa mixture and adequate curing time will ensure the success of your project. Don't cut corners, and take your time with curing. The materials you mix into the planter will determine its density. Also important is that the longer hypertufa cures, the stronger it will be. Read these instructions carefully before proceeding to the steps to form your planter.

Mixing Hypertufa

You'll mix a batch of cementlike material called hypertufa by combining ingredients, including Portland cement and peat moss. The recipe you use depends on what you plan to make from hypertufa. Adding fiberglass fibers to the mixture produces a strong material ideal for medium to large containers. Or, instead, stir in sand, which is appropriate for molding smaller items that might hold water. Because we're making a large planter, we'll opt for fiberglass, mixing a handful of fibers with Portland cement, sifted peat moss, and perlite.

Always choose Portland cement. It does not contain gravel, which can produce a coarse finish and will weaken the project. You'll find fiberglass fibers at most building stores or check a concrete or masonry supply center. Another note: Before mixing peat moss, be sure to strain it with a sieve, or sift it through hardware cloth to remove twigs and clumps from the smooth material you want to use in your hypertufa mix. Hypertufa dries looking like concrete, and you can add powered concrete dye to your mix for color.

Drying and Curing

Hypertufa takes at least a couple of days to dry and several weeks to completely cure. This curing process requires patience and is important for achieving a characteristic aged look. Don't rush it. After allowing hypertufa to dry for at least 48 hours, remove the forms. Because hypertufa's aged look is manufactured, go ahead and knock off the corners of your planter with a hammer, or use a screwdriver to create grooves in the surface. Now is the time to make your mark.

Next, cure hypertufa by wrapping the planter in plastic and placing it in a cool area for about one month. Then, unwrap the planter and allow it to sit outside, uncovered for several weeks. Periodically rinse the planter with water to lessen its alkalinity, which will harm plants. You may add vinegar to your water mix to hasten this process.

Next, cure the planter for one more week in a dry, inside area. You'll notice that the fiberglass fibers produce hairy bristles on the hypertufa surface. A propane torch burns these off in a hurry. Do not hold the torch in one spot for more than a couple seconds, and be sure the planter is completely dry. If the torch heats up a water pocket, the pocket could explode and blow a hole in your planter.

Finally, apply a coat of masonry sealer to basins and pieces that must hold water.

WEATHERED LOOKING
hypertufa complements a
rustic garden space.

REPRO: SILO SO YELLOW SCREEN
APPEARS IN BKD

Preliminaries

You can build any shape or size form for hypertufa from polystyrene, or you can use a trusty planter turned upside down as a mold. Simply cover it in plastic before covering it in hypertufa mix. Forms can also be made from plywood. Or, you can even build a mound of sand or soil, cover it in plastic, and use this free-form shape as a base for your planter.

Supplies

- **Tape measure**
- **Jigsaw**
- **Straightedge**
- **Drill**
- **Hacksaw**
- **Wheelbarrow or mixing trough**
- **Hammer**
- **Chisel or paint scraper**
- **Wire brush**
- **Propane torch**
- **12-quart bucket**
- **2" (5.1 cm) polystyrene insulation board (4' x 8' [122 x 244 cm] sheet)**
- **3½" (89 mm) deck screws**
- **Duct tape**
- **4" diameter (10.2 cm) PVC pipe (4" [10.2 cm])**
- **Dust mask**
- **Gloves**
- **Plastic tarp**
- **Scrap 2 x 4**
- **Portland cement**
- **Sifted peat moss**
- **Perlite**
- **Fiberglass fibers**
- **Powdered cement dye (optional)**

Cutting List

Outer Form
- **22" x 32" (55.9 x 81.3 cm) = Floor**
- **11" x 32" (27.9 x 81.3 cm) = Sides**
- **11" x 18" (27.9 x 45.7 cm) = Ends**

Inner Form
- **7" x 24" (17.8 x 61 cm) = Sides**
- **7" x 10" (17.8 x 25.4 cm) = Ends and center support**

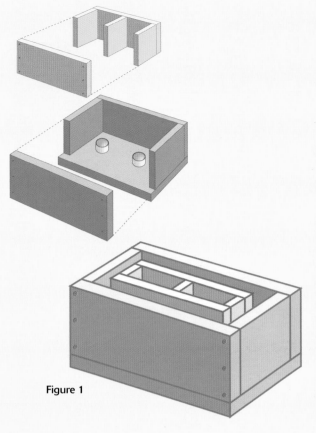

Figure 1

Steps

1. Measure, mark and use a jigsaw to cut pieces of polystyrene insulation board to size from the cutting list. Construct the outer form by fitting an end piece between two side pieces. Fasten joints using deck screws. Repeat for other end. Wrap duct tape around each end to secure the side and end pieces. Attach the bottom by placing it on top of your rectangle. Screw and tape the bottom in place. Construct the inner form in the same manner, with the addition of a center support. Cut two 2" (5.1-cm) pieces of PVC pipe and set aside **(Figure 1)**.

2. Mix the hypertufa in a mixing trough. Use 2 parts Portland cement, 3 parts sifted peat moss, 3 parts perlite, and one handful of fiberglass fibers. Mix the dry ingredients thoroughly. Add water gradually. The hypertufa is ready when you can squeeze a little water from a handfull. Wear a dust mask and gloves while handling and working with hypertufa.

Cure hypertufa in a shady spot. Bright sunlight will cure hypertufa unevenly, causing it to crack and fracture.

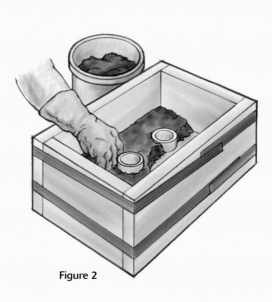

Figure 2

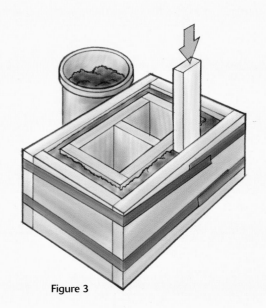

Figure 3

3. Press the PVC pipe pieces into the floor of the outer form to form the planter's drainage holes. Firmly pack hypertufa into the floor of the form, working around PVC. Continue this process until floor is solid and 2" (5.1 cm) thick **(Figure 2).**

4. Place inner form inside outer form. Add hypertufa between the outer and inner forms to create a wall. Use a scrap 2 x 4 to firmly pack down material. Continue this process until hypertufa is level with the top of the forms **(Figure 3).**

5. Cover planter with a plastic tarp and allow it to dry. In especially warm weather, prevent cracking by misting the planter with water occasionally. After at least 48 hours, remove tape and screws from the outer form. Check walls for dryness; be sure they will stand on their own before removing the form completely. Next, remove inner forms.

6. Allow planter to dry and cure according to the *Drying and Curing* section, on page 98. Remove hairy fringe from fiberglass fibers with a torch.

7. Encourage moss growth by brushing buttermilk on the planter. Press patches of fresh moss onto the surface, and mist with water.

PROJECT PAIRINGS

THESE PROJECTS WILL COMPLEMENT your hypertufa planter:

Window Boxes

Wake up to the smell of fresh flowers, and grow herbs within arm's reach of the kitchen. Window boxes are handy, hanging gardens that add a punch of color and cottage appeal to a home, and they are ideal for courtyard properties that lack ample planting room. You can fill window boxes with annuals, create theme gardens, or drop potted plants inside of them. Window boxes hung on a backyard shed can make it look like a guesthouse.

Start this afternoon project with a trip to the lumber yard or home improvement store, where you can find the basic carpentry supplies necessary to complete this project.

The Dirt

As with any garden, the size of your window box should accommodate the plants you choose and the size of the window it will grace. Be sure to allow space for plants to spread out as they grow, and if you decide to place pots in the window box instead of filling it with soil and treating it as a planter, make the window box tall enough to conceal the entire pot.

Because creating a window box involves converting wood pieces into a weather-ready outdoor home for plants, opt for rot-resistant wood, such as cedar or redwood. And take care to complete the finishing touches of this project, as they are critical to plant health. Your window box needs drainage holes and landscape fabric to prevent soil loss. Add to your window box's life expectancy by buying metal or plastic liners. Finally, play with the decorative possibilities by painting the window box to coordinate with your home.

Preliminaries

This project is constructed from five, cut pieces and measurements are based on a standard, single window. The box length should be ¾ of an inch (2 cm) wider than the interior wall studs that frame the window. Generally, wall studs are 16 inches (40.6 cm) apart, so the total length of the window box for a standard, single window is 32¾ inches (83 cm). If your box must fit a double window, measure the window's width from one outside edge of the trim to the other. This is the length of your box. The same rule applies to custom windows. Simply alter the cutting measurements to accommodate your window size. It's a good idea to treat this cutting guide as a map for your project. Photocopy the page and make notes on it so you can reconfigure this project to fit any size window on your home.

If the window box tips when hung, you can add a spacer to keep the box perpindicular to your house. Simply attach a strip of scrap wood to the back of the window box.

Supplies

- **4-foot 1 x 6 (121.9 x 1.9 x 14 cm) (1)**
- **8-foot 1 x 8 (243.8 x 1.9 x 19 cm) (1)**
- **Saw**
- **Drill**
- **¾" (19 mm) drill bit**
- **Wood glue**
- **Sand paper**
- **Landscape fabric**
- **Nonstaining deck screws**
- **Screwdriver**
- **Hooks and eye screws (at least 1½" [3.8 cm])**
- **Natural sealant, such as linseed oil or beeswax**
- **Exterior paint (your color choice)**

Steps

1. From the 1 x 8, cut the front and back to 33 ½" (1.9 x 19 x 85.1 cm). From the 1 x 6, cut the bottom to 33 ½" (1.9 x 14 x 85.1 cm) and the ends to 6 ¾" (1.9 x 14 x 17.1 cm).

If you are customizing these pieces, the bottom piece the same length as the front and back, but narrower. Cut the two ends to the same width as the bottom of the piece. Figure the height of the side pieces by subtracting the thickness of the bottom piece from the height of the sides. Note: save scraps for spacers if you hang the box.

2. On the long sides of the front and back pieces, ⅜" (1 cm) in from one edge, mark points ½" from each end and every 8" (20.3 cm) in between. Drill a ³⁄₃₂" (20 mm) pilot hole at each point and drive a deck screw partially into the hole.

3. Apply wood glue to one edge of the bottom piece. Press together the bottom and side piece (making an L shape), then drive the screws. Repeat for other side piece to form a U shape.

4. Dry fit the ends to check for size and adjust if necessary. Apply a bead of wood glue to the

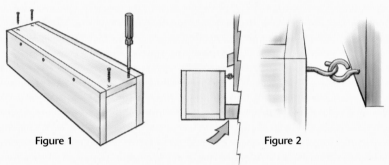

Figure 1

Figure 2

three inside edges at each U end. Slip the end pieces into the U. Drill pilot holes and drive two deck screws through each side and the bottom into the ends **(Figure 1).**

5. Drill several ¾" (19 mm) drainage holes in the bottom of the window box.

6. Sand the outside of the box to smooth rough edges. Line the interior of the box with a layer of landscape fabric to prevent soil from running out of the drainage holes.

7. Hang the box. Find wall studs that frame the window. On a standard window, mark the center of the windowsill, measure 16" (40.5 cm) to the right and left. Mark these spots. Measure 1" (2.5 cm) below the marks. Drill holes for screw hooks here. Drill at a slight upward angle, then finish by screwing in hooks. Use the shaft of the screwdriver to assist in twisting the hooks in. Attach the eye bolts to your window box to align with the hooks **(Figure 2).**

PROJECT PAIRINGS

NOW THAT YOUR WINDOW BOXES are sitting pretty, try these related projects:

Container Planting Clinic

Practical, portable, and perfectly poised for small spaces, container gardens are an ideal planting solution for cramped gardeners and fickle flower lovers. If your property is short in the square-footage department, no problem. You can surely find room to squeeze in a trio of potted plants, which will infuse an intimate courtyard or porch with color. Also, containers are far less of a commitment than plant beds. Use them as a test lab to experiment with exciting, new annuals or interesting tropicals. Foodies who like to grow their own herbs will appreciate containers for their versatility.

Containers nestle comfortably in plant beds, and rest easy on patios. Because you can constantly reposition them, as long as light exposure is adequate for chosen plants, you'll never grow bored with these moveable minigardens. And today, the word "container" is relative. Your choices extend beyond typical ceramic pots: any shell capable of holding soil and draining water is fair game.

The Dirt

A container garden is an ideal afternoon project. It doesn't take long to create and will add impact to a space. But success depends on appropriate soil, sunlight, and plant placement. Also, you should understand some design principles before you choose the subjects of your portable garden. As you follow the steps to create your container garden, consider these factors.

Select Soil

Think of your container as a Lilliputian plant bed—a pint-sized garden. In any planting area, container or bed, soil is essential for providing plants the nutrients they need to grow and thrive. Because you have the opportunity to mix up your own foundation for plants in a somewhat controlled environment, you should start with the best possible soil. That is a combination of peat,

soil, and sand. Or, mix two parts potting soil and one part compost, which will add body and nutrients to the mix. Do not transfer topsoil from your backyard to a pot. Heavy, clay material will not allow oxygen and water to reach plant roots.

You can purchase quality soil at garden centers and retail stores, but always check the contents on the bag for those three elements. Also, choose a brand that already contains fertilizer. Of course, you'll want to apply a slow-release fertilizer after planting, so the container plants receive a gradual, constant flow of nutrients, but for now, we're just talking soil.

Partner Like-Minded Plants

Plants with similar water and light needs will grow in harmony. Mix a shade-dwelling plant in a pot with sun lovers, and you've got a game of *Survivor*. Plants that thrive in sun will overwhelm the shade variety. Think compatibility when choosing plants. Their tags will indicate light and water needs, and you should pay attention to both. You wouldn't want to drown a cactus by pairing it with impatiens, which need daily watering when planted in containers.

That said, also consider where you will place containers before filling them with plant material. If you plan to move them around, select hardy plants that will succeed in shady and sunny areas. If you know a container will rest in a spot with full sun, and then choose plants accordingly. In this case, all plants that you install in the container should be sun-lovers. You get the idea.

Build Layers

The key design principle for containers is to plant in tiers. Aim for three stories of plant material: a tall focal point, a middle section with rich foliage, and trailing varieties that cascade down the side of a pot. This will provide depth and texture to your container planting—layers of interest.

Vertical appeal is critical. Choose the centerpiece first, and work around it. You may opt for a dwarf conifer (if you have a large pot), or perennials with height. Pick plants with lots of foliage and/or blooms for the middle tier. This will add body to your design. Ivy and herbs, such as thyme, are your third tier. They will roll over the edges of a container and soften the look.

Now a note on technique: When planting layers, start in the middle and work your way out toward the edge of the container for 360-degree appeal. However, if you know you'll

position the container against a wall or other backdrop, you can build your tiers by starting in the front and working toward edges. Think of how you might decorate a Christmas tree that you push against a wall. Why bother with ornaments on the unexposed area? Same goes for containers. Position plants where they'll earn the second look and compliments they deserve.

Uncontained Possibilities

If it can hold soil and has a hole in the bottom for water drainage, it's a viable container for plants. Boots, bicycle baskets, urns, watering cans, bird baths, wheelbarrows, antique bowls, even bathtubs—as long as the "planter" doesn't retain water, which promotes root rot and disease, you can use it as a landscape

A CREATIVE flower-pot dog adds whimsy to a back yard.

Don't limit yourself to a single container. A cluster of potted gardens adds as much impact as a flower bed. Line them along balconies, arrange them in the corner of a patio space, or flank them on your front porch.

feature. Scout out potential containers in your attic, antique shops, or the hardware store. Clear plastic liners you can purchase at a garden store will protect the container if you don't want to spoil it with soil.

Preliminaries

Before you begin, consider the size of the container and your soil needs. Most plants will not need more than 8 inches (20.3 cm) of soil to accommodate roots and growth. If you are working with a robust ceramic 20-inch (50.8-cm) -deep container, filling the whole pot with dirt will take away the portability that potted plants offer. The container will get too heavy. This is where an upturned plastic potting container comes in handy. Flip a plastic potting container upside down and place it in the container. It will serve as a shelf. Fill in dirt, and you'll not only get the drainage you need, but your container won't be heavy like a cement block. Or, if you prefer, use clay shards from broken pots as filler. This will also provide drainage and fill space, though you'll want to avoid this material if your container is already heavy. You can use Styrofoam packing peanuts, but be sure you do not confuse them for the new degradable cornstarch pellets, which will eventually turn to mush in the bottom of a moist pot.

Also, you'll want to decide if you will place your container indoors or outside. Location dictates plant choice. If you want to create a container that you can enjoy outside in the summer, and rescue from winter weather by keeping it indoors when the temperature drops, you should consider ways to "change out" plantings. Replace annuals with herbs

when you move the container to your kitchen for the winter. Or, add a fern as a middle tier, which will thrive inside. Because container plantings provide so many options, take your time in the nursery and peruse plant stock.

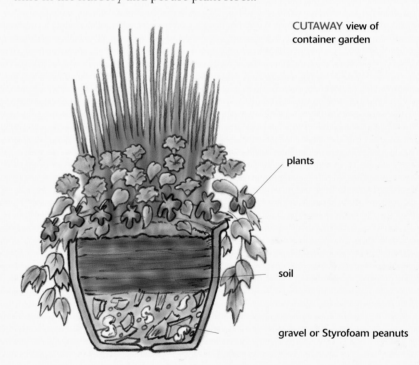

CUTAWAY view of container garden

plants

soil

gravel or Styrofoam peanuts

Supplies

- **Container**
- **Plastic liner (optional)**
- **Gravel or Styrofoam peanuts**
- **Soil mix**
- **Plants (three tiers)**

Protect plants from mealy bugs and spider mites (which you'll notice by webs that dangle from foliage), and keep leaves shiny by cleaning foliage with a spray bottle mix of dish soap and water.

Steps

1. Prepare a container. Make sure your container has at least one drainage hole. Larger containers need additional holes. Protect your container with a plastic liner if desired. Be sure your hole punctures this layer, as well.

2. Spread a thin layer of gravel or Styrofoam peanuts on the bottom of the container. This will ensure proper drainage and prevent soil from compacting near holes and clogging the area where water can escape. If your container does not drain properly, plants can suffer from root rot.

3. Add a layer of soil mix. Use a soil-sand-peat prepackaged mix that contains fertilizer, or mix your own, using two parts soil, one part compost.

4. Position plants in tiers. Assuming you will place the container in an area where it will be exposed at all angles, start planting in the center. Place your tallest plant in the middle. Follow with a second tier of leafy, colorful plants. These need not be the same variety. Just ensure they are shorter than your vertical centerpiece plant. Finally, plant a ring of trailing plants around the first and second tiers. Be sure to position plants so they are spaced apart and have room to grow. While your container might look sparse at first, plants will quickly fill in. When you crowd plants, they compete for water and nutrients. The result is a pot filled with weaker plants, rather than a container with several, lush varieties with strong roots that had space to mature.

5. Add more soil, until it reaches about 2 inches (5.1 cm) from the top of the container. Gently pat down soil.

6. Water in your container plants, until you notice water seeping from drainage holes. This ensures that water is reaching roots. Allow moisture to absorb. If water is gone in an hour, you've watered your container just enough. If you notice water standing several hours later, you overwatered. Take care to check containers for dryness on a daily basis, especially if they sit in the sun. Stem and leaf wilt signal dehydration, but you should not let plants get to this point. Other signs are slow leaf growth, transparent leaves, flowers that drop prematurely, or curling, yellowed lower leaves.

So, how much water is enough? Unfortunately, there is no easy way to answer this question. The best watering advice is to observe carefully, and start by reading plant tags that indicate water requirements. Do avoid frequent watering in small amounts, which can force air from soil and result in disease and rotting. It's better to water deep so moisture reaches roots; then stick your finger in the soil periodically to check moisture level and act accordingly.

NOTICE THE VERTICAL interest in this container, which makes use of a recycled tire.

PROJECT PAIRINGS

COMPLEMENT containers with these projects:

Install Drip Irrigation Set up water works in your containers.	48
Herb Garden Steal these ideas for your container planting.	94
Window Boxes A close cousin of the container garden	102

PROJECT

Cool, Creative Planters

If it can contain soil, tolerate Mother Nature, hold plants, and stand a few pokes in the bottom for drainage, it can certainly serve as a container for flowers. Sure, you could purchase sturdy terra-cotta planters at the garden center, and the plastic ones available weather nicely and mimic just about any surface you can imagine. But different is good. And because landscaping is a personal expression in green, a way to make your mark on the land and define it as yours, then you should explore options outside of planter standards.

So, don't be contained by the word "container." Think outside of the planter.

Surprising artifacts transform into useful, unusual containers. Boots, baskets, urns, antique bowls, vintage bathtubs, even old-school commodes (nonworking, of course) can convert into whimsical planters. Why not park an old truck in a garden if your property is in a rural environment? A truck bed brimming with flowers says "country farmer's market," and who's to argue about the out-of-commission automobile if your neighbors aren't within view?

With a few easy steps, you can turn just about any item capable of holding something into a expressive container. We'll show you how to do it here. And don't hesitate to steal the ideas from page 111.

Supplies
- **Interesting item capable of holding soil**
- **Drill or awl**
- **Plastic liner**
- **Landscape fabric or coco fiber**

Steps
1. To allow for drainage in a solid container, use a drill or awl to make holes.

2. To prevent excessive leakage in containers such as baskets, line the interior with landscape fabric or coco fiber.

3. Plant according to instructions in Planting Clinic Container, page 104.

PROJECT PAIRINGS

CREATIVE CONTAINERS complement these projects:

THIS ANTIQUE TRUCK parked in a field landscape adds country charm to the property.

COILED ROPE around a plain old planter refinishes a basic container into one with cowboy appeal, perfect for cactus.

THIS URN displays flowers as if they are planted atop a silver platter.

A PAIR OF OLD SHOES, once soiled from outdoor play, are now filled with soil and serve as a quirky holder.

Ivy Topiary

If your prefer tidy over untamed, and manicured over messy, a topiary planting is a suitable selection for your space. In a way, topiary is the poodle haircut of shrubs. But the angular, clean appeal is artistic and lends itself to geometric garden designs.

You can achieve this look with a shortcut: create an ivy topiary from mature plants. The interesting container feature complements formal patio settings, or add a partner and flank your front door with two, eye-catching topiaries. We'll show you how to get results fast.

The Dirt

Topiaries grow as fast as any plant, but you must be careful to trim them regularly so they don't lose their painstakingly neat shapes. The risk you take when trimming existing shrubs into unnatural forms is that excessive pruning, which is necessary for topiaries, can block light and oxygen from the center of the shrub. The result is an ornamental with lots of leaves on the surface, but nothing but naked branches in the guts of the shrub. In the long term, this is not especially beneficial for plants.

However, with proper plant nutrition—water, healthy soil, and fertilization—shrub topiaries will thrive in their sculpted forms. Topiaries that are pruned regularly, and this may mean weekly depending on the weather and type of plant, will look like living statues in a garden.

This particular project involves manipulating ivy into a three-tiered topiary. Using a wire frame, the trailing plant clings and grows to this form, therefore avoiding the pruning health problem discussed earlier. Pruning regularly and never allowing ivy to exceed 3 inches (7.6 cm) encourages branching. This refers to offshoot growth that develop from pruned branch tips. The result: a rich, green topiary with interesting texture, thanks to ivy's distinct foliage.

SYMMETRICAL, MANICURED TOPIARY must be trimmed weekly. Its conservative appeal is ideal for landscapes.

Preliminaries

You can find ivy in garden centers at almost any time of year. For instant gratification with this project, purchase mature hanging baskets of ivy that have about two dozen hanging stems. This plant will serve as the base inside the topiary frames. For more information on ivies, see *Healthy Choices* on page 89.

Supplies

- **Large planting container**
- **Potting soil**
- **Gravel (for drainage)**
- **Wire topiary frames; two circles and a base**
- **One mature hanging basket of ivy**

Steps

1. Prepare the container by spreading a layer of gravel for drainage and adding potting soil. Remove the ivy from the hanging basket and transfer to the container. (For more specific directions, see page 109.)

2. Assemble the wire frame according to directions. Poke the base into the planting container and attach one wire frame globe shape.

3. Wind the inner strands of the ivy around the wire frame. Allow the outer strands to drape over the side of the container.

4. After the ivy growth reaches the first globe frame, remove the leaves from the trunk area of the topiary.

5. Continue to train the ivy by trimming shoots that exceed 3"(7.6 cm). This will encourage branching and lush growth so ivy will fill the topiary frame.

Rock Garden

Convert a flat property that lacks texture or character into an enticing, layered landscape with the help of a rock garden. This project is ideal for front entry areas, spaces adjacent to plant beds, and sloped yards. Also, rock gardens provide interest in places where plant material and turf resist growth. Varying colors of stone, rugged and smooth surfaces, and stones of different shapes create a garden of contrasts. The result is a contemplative setting, a miniature mountain range with plants peeking through a rock arrangement.

Rock gardens can be small or large. They can comfortably fit into small landscapes, and you only need to reserve a 4- to 6-foot (1.2- to 1.8-m) -diameter corner to make an impact. This project will guide you through steps to build a small rock garden, though you can apply these principles to any size outcropping you design.

The Dirt

The trickiest part about creating a rock garden is placement. Sounds easy enough. But actually, most homeowners who attempt rock gardens do not consider the size, shape, and color of rocks before arranging them. You don't want the rock to look like it has fallen out of the sky and landed in your back yard. Your goal is for rocks to look as though Mother Nature herself placed them there. Rock placement should be intentional and well thought out. Plants and rocks should not collide in the garden, but instead exist harmoniously, despite the contrast of texture.

So think of your rock garden as a puzzle. Separate rocks you will use into piles, and examine their colors, textures, shapes, and sizes. You wouldn't create a perimeter of rocks by lining up all the large pieces, then grouping the small pieces at one end. Alternate shapes and sizes to add interest. Notice how rocks interlock, how their grooves support and hold one another in place when arranged with a careful eye. Consider this technique when working through the steps in this project.

Rock Selection

The rock you incorporate into your garden will depend largely on where you live and what materials you can access. Of course, there are suppliers who distribute and ship rock, and you can contact a local landscape company and ask for references.

You can always find free rocks by searching construction sites for upturned stones with unusual or attractive qualities. Or, visit a quarry and handpick your own stones. You will find a generous selection, and go home with high-quality beautiful rock for your garden.

When choosing rock, keep in mind its porosity. You can tell by its mass: the heavier the rock for its size, the more dense it is. Porous rocks weather more quickly, forming a mossy patina that gives the impression that they are veterans in your landscape, not stark brand-new additions. However, depending on the look you want to achieve, and the size of rocks you plan to use (boulders or stones), you may choose among varieties such as these:

Red sandstone: Porous with an attractive red color. Crumbly rock looks weathered. Use chips as mulch to prevent weed growth in your rock garden.

Moss rock: Dense, thin sandstone, dark in color and ideal for retaining walls.

Weathered limestone: Sedimentary rock available in small or larger pieces, and boulders.

Lava rock: This porous rock is lightweight and contrasts nicely with white gravel. Artistic shapes serve as accent pieces. Select them individually from a quarry. Because quarries charge by pound, purchase these rocks in warmer weather when they don't contain frozen water that can double their weight.

Plant Picks

When choosing plants, your first decision is whether your rock garden will emulate a dry rocky outcropping or a cool and wet alpine meadow. The first requires plants that like dry heat and well drained soil. The second is geared more toward alpine plants and mosses. Rock gardens of both types are very popular, so garden center staff will be able to assist you in plant selection.

Foliage plants will provide year-round color and soften the look of your rock garden. Combine low-growing, clumping varieties such as hens and chicks (*Sempervivum tectorum*) with taller leafy plants like lamb's ears (*Stachys byzantina*). Add annuals for color, and stick to a theme instead of planting a mish-mash of plant material. Remember, you want the outcropping to look like an act of nature, not an accident.

When choosing plants, keep in mind your climate zone (refer to the USDA Plant Hardiness Map on page 215), and select hardy varieties that are well suited to your particular rock garden. Ground covers and low-growing foliage are good choices. Even in a sunny, dry rock garden you can grow moss on the shady side of the rocks. By growing moss, you'll give rocks a weathered, established look like they've been there for years Finally, annuals can add a shot of color in season, but be sure to coordinate colors to complement the rock.

Preliminaries

Assuming that you'll start this project from scratch, you need to pick a plot and clear the area. This spot may be flat, so you'll build up the earth. Or, you can position your outcropping on an existing slope or terrace area that would benefit from a more formal rock setting. Choose a shady place that will promote growth of moss and similar rockery plantings. Remove the turf, or simply place newspaper on the turf, and pile soil on top. The newspaper will choke the turf, eventually causing it to decompose and protecting your rock garden from sprouting weeds. Now, you are ready to collect supplies and begin building a small, 5- foot (1.5-m) -diameter rock garden.

Supplies

- **Rocks of your choice**
- **Plants of your choice**
- **Soil**
- **Wheelbarrow**
- **Mulch**
- **Planting supplies** (page 31)

Steps

1. After clearing the area and arranging rocks, as suggested in The Dirt, select rocks to serve as the first layer of your garden. Note: Reserve attractive and unusual rocks for the second layer and for accent rocks. Choose larger rocks for the first ring, and place them in a circlular shape **(Figure 1)**.

2. Next, create a platform for planting. You need a compacted base underneath your rock-work so it won't shift over time from freeze and thaw cycles. You'll do this by filling in the rock perimeter with sandy soil, which will promote drainage. If your soil is clay, you'll want to amend it (refer to Cottage Garden Master Plan, page 76). Compact soil so it is firm enough to support rocks without sinking, but not so packed that you can't plant.

3. Lay the second layer of rocks, paying attention to the rocks' natural grooves and character. Form a circle within a circle.

4. Begin placing plants. Alternate planting and placing rocks. You want the effect to be that of a natural outcropping where plants peek through rocks. Save the smaller rocks for this "filler" placement **(Figure 2)**.

5. Finally, suppress weeds with mulch, but don't just use any mulch. Traditional bark mulches look out of place. Instead, use stone mulch purchased at a nursery that matches the color of main rocks, or pebble that has chipped off of rocks you chose for your garden.

Figure 1

Figure 2

PROJECT PAIRINGS

ROCK GARDENS partner well with these projects:

Drought-Tolerant Landscape   80
Discover other time-saving alternatives to caring for turf.

Interlock Retaining Wall   150
Apply your rock knowledge to this more advanced project.

PROJECT

Zen Space

For peace of mind and a spiritual escape, create a Zen garden as a quiet, serene area of your outdoor space. Zen gardens are rich in history, dating back to the late 6th century when Buddhist priests would stroll a *kansho-niwa*, or contemplative garden, and hold tea ceremonies in tranquil, symbolic settings. Every detail in a Zen garden is mindful and significant, positioned to provoke thought. Raked pebble paths represent flowing water, and a single large rock signifies a mountain towering over a countryside. Contrasting lush, green foliage with meandering paths take visitors on a journey. Waterfalls and statues provide meaningful points of interest along the way.

You can opt for authentic Zen, which is actually a rather stark landscape. Or, you can draw from Zen principles and modify them to create your own version of the serene contemplation garden. You don't need a large property—even a corner will do for this project.

The Dirt

We associate certain elements with Zen: the obvious Buddha sculpture, bamboo, white gravel pathways, rectangular reflecting pools, and linear paths. The purpose of a Zen garden is to tell a story, to lead visitors on a spiritual path with observation points that challenge the mind. The most popular type of Zen garden is called *karesansui*, meaning dry-mountain-and-water garden. Zen priests used *shakkei* (borrowed scenery) when designing their gardens, drawing inspiration from distant mountains and views. True Zen gardens are simple, pure, and subtle, but powerful in meaning.

Following are typical characteristics of a Zen garden:

A story: Every element is a part of the story your garden tells. The garden should challenge your mind as you enter it, walk its path, and consider the purpose of every element.

Contemplation: Include places to sit and ponder.

Contrast: This concept is the defining feature of a Zen garden. For example, dark lava rock positioned as outcroppings near a white gravel path, carefully raked in a wave pattern. Contrast is accomplished with texture (foliage and rocks), color (black and white, or green plants against a stark white gravel background), and positioning of elements.

Simplicity: Think clear mind, free spirit, and purity. Zen gardens are not cluttered or whimsical like cottage gardens or wild flower beds. They are minimalist, and therefore especially complementary to a contemporary style home.

Preliminaries

As with any garden project, the first step is to choose an appropriate setting. You may want to incorporate contemplative principals of Zen design in front of your home, so guests walk a journey through a thought-provoking setting before reaching your door. Or, perhaps your Zen garden is a retreat in your backyard, consuming a modest plot by a water feature or adjacent to a patio space.

Most Zen gardens have a foundation of gravel, stone, or pebble, so you'll first need to clear turf from the area and prepare the spot by laying landscape fabric to discourage weeds. Another preparatory consideration is privacy. Shield this garden from foot traffic and hustle-bustle zones. For example, if you decide to create the garden near a driveway, garage, or children's play space, plan on creating a privacy fence from bamboo, or plant trees that will block disruptive views.

Finally, plant selection is critical as you plan your Zen design. This is not the space to sample the latest rainbow palette of annuals. Again, think simple and structured for visual interest and contemplation.

Some plant suggestions include:
- **Red-leaf Japanese maple,** *Acer palmatum 'Atropurpureum'*
- **Dwarf bamboo,** *Pleioblastus fortunei*
- **Creeping juniper,** *Juniperus horizontalis*
- **Spreading cotoneaster,** *Cotoneaster divaricatus*
- **Azalea,** *Rhododendron*
- **Hemlock,** *Tsuga*
- **Flowering cherry,** *Prunus*
- **Dogwood,** *Cornus*
- **Ferns,** *Cheilanthes*
- **Bigleaf hostas,** *Hosta montana*
- **Pine varieties**

Supplies
- **Pea gravel or pebble stone**
- **Large feature rocks**
- **Landscape fabric**
- **Plant material**
- **Stepping stones or pathway**
- **Entrance**
- **Contemplative features, such as statuary or a pond**
- **Sitting area**
- **Planting supplies** (page 31)
- **Wheelbarrow**

Some types of bamboo (especially *Phyllostachys aurea*) are extremely aggressive, invasive plants. It is important to contain any spreading bamboo variety with a collar. This looks like plastic edging, and it is about 3 feet (1 m) deep. The collar serves as a planter, in a sense. You dig a hole for the collar then plant the bamboo within it. This way its roots cannot extend beyond the collar, so it will not take over your Zen garden. Of course, before installing any plant, be sure your climate will support it. Bamboo will not thrive in climates where temperatures drop below 20°F (-7°C).

Steps (See opposite page.)

1. Choose an entry point for the garden. This may consist of two parallel trees that frame the view of your space, or you can plant a row of shielding bamboo, leaving an opening for an entry. Another option is a traditional toreii gate, or similar wrought iron design with simple lines.

2. Clear a space for your garden, as described in Preliminaries. Lay down stone or gravel, symbolizing flowing water. Rake gravel into a swirling pattern to emulate waves.

3. Create a meandering pathway through the garden, along which you will place features, artistic rocks, and plantings.

4. Place large feature rocks. A single, large rock makes a statement. Do not clutter the area. Continue placing rocks and features with the philosophy that each is a stopping point for meditation. An alternative to feature rocks is sculpture as a focal point.

5. Add plantings from the suggested list. Plant material that will contrast with gravel and rock, and also protect the serene space.

6. You may opt for a bamboo fence, which you can purchase ready-made or make yourself by buying loose bamboo.

7. Place a bench for quiet contemplation.

PROJECT PAIRINGS

REFER TO THESE PROJECTS as you construct a Zen garden:

PART FOUR

Form & Function

What's practical is pleasing. The most livable, visually appealing landscapes include elements that enhance the usability of the space. For what good is an amazing back yard if you cannot touch, feel, and enjoy it? We need points of access, places to sit, covers for protection, and solutions for masking undesirable views. Yes, you can be funky and functional, pretty and practical. The projects in this section merge beauty and the basics.

Lay a Path

Pathways guide visitors through your land-scape, drawing the eye to focal points and leading them from point A to point B. Functional and aesthetic, stepping stones act as a divider, breaking up large areas into usable quadrants for gardening, entertaining, or outdoor play. Pathways also unify projects that seem like distant cousins—joining a stranded pond with a nearby garden, or partnering a lonely plant bed with a nearby patio. Paths connect the dots. In addition, you'll control foot traffic if you create a clear route through your lawn.

Sharpen your skills here by learning how to install a basic, stone pathway, then let your imagination guide you and experiment with different surfaces. There are lots of options.

The Dirt

Laying a path requires some forward thinking. Once you dig out a hole of turf to hold a paver, stepping stone, or other hardscape material, you leave a gap in your lawn. You'll fill the clearing when you install the surface of your choice, but if you decide that the placement isn't quite right, you're left with a bald spot.

That said, consider these questions before deciding where to place your pathway:

- **What do you want** visitors to notice in your outdoor space?
- **What features** must you travel to before enjoying?
- **Are there areas** where turf growth is a problem and an alternative surface would look more appealing?
- **Does your yard** contain landscape features that don't seem to connect?
- **If your turf** was a moat of water, what bridge would you need to reach your favorite spot?

Preliminaries

Map out your pathway on your site plan (see page 17) before beginning this project. As you look at the diagram of your yard, consider the preceding questions you answered, and pencil in a line or lines to connect features. This line represents a potential pathway. Now is the time to play around with placement options.

When laying stepping stones, be sure to set them on a bed of gravel or sand to provide proper drainage.

Figure 1

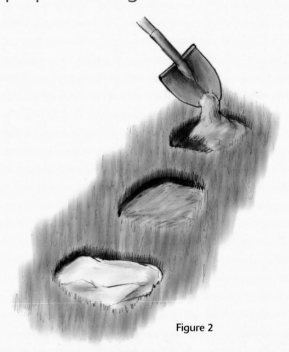

Figure 2

Walk the path you diagrammed and take note of your stride. How much space do you need between each stepping stone? While walking the proposed pathway, sprinkle some flour on each footstep. This will provide a rough placement guide for stepping stones.

Test out different placements by cutting out cardboard pieces shaped like the stone you plan to use. Create circles, squares, or misshapen pieces sized to match the stepping stones you plan to purchase.

Supplies
- Spade or garden shovel
- Sand or compactable gravel
- Stepping stones

Steps

1. Place stones in the desired pathway, after testing options using cardboard cutouts.

2. Allow stepping stones to rest in place for several days to kill the grass underneath, providing an outline for excavation (**Figure 1**).

3. Using a spade or garden shovel, cut around the outline of each stepping stone, then excavate the area. Refer to the stone thickness as your guide. You want stones to be flush with the ground once installed. To allow room for a layer of sand or gravel, which stabilizes the stepping stone, dig each hole 2 inches (5.1 cm) deeper than the thickness of the stones. Spread sand in each hole.

4. Place stones in sand-filled holes. Sand serves as grout, filling in small gaps between the hole you dug and surrounding turf. Add or remove sand to ensure each stepping stone is secure (**Figure 2**).

PROJECT PAIRINGS

TO MAKE A PERFECT PATH, try these projects:

Make Your Own Stepping Stones   **126**
Personalize your pathway.

Install Bed Edging   **128**
While you're working with stone material, add a neat trim to plant beds.

Make Your Own Stepping Stones

There's nothing like homemade, and this applies not only to baked goods and greeting cards, but also to decorative accents for the outdoors. As you grow more comfortable with landscaping techniques and begin to design your space to complement your family's lifestyle, you'll seek ways to customize basic materials. Stepping stones are one way to personalize a pathway or garden. Turn the project into a family affair and create memory stones with children's handprints. Experiment with cement colorants, or embed mosaic tiles, fancy glass pebbles, and cookie cutters into the surface. Stick with a theme, or create each stone as an individual artwork. These stepping stones also make great house-warming gifts and show true character.

MAKING YOUR OWN stepping stones is much more affordable than purchasing pavers. The best part: you can incorporate your personality with decorative touches.

Cement is caustic and can cause burns on exposed skin. Wear rubber gloves and protect your eyes from splatters with safety goggles.

The Dirt

Handmade stepping stones are easy as pie, and you may find the materials you need for the project in your own kitchen. Cake pans are ideal molds. Of course, you'll want to choose materials you don't plan to use again for baking, or purchase disposable aluminum cake pans for the project.

Because you'll use cement mix, which sets fairly quickly, gather materials for your project in advance. Cookie cutters in different shapes and letters can serve as stencils, or you can draw freehand designs using a popsicle stick or chopsticks as drawing tools. Try embedding some of these adornments—marbles, glass beads, fish tank gravel, decorative sand, mosaic tile, broken pieces of pottery.

Keep in mind, you'll be stepping on these stones. So choose materials with a smooth surface, or plan to smooth rough edges with sandpaper (especially for broken pottery accents).

Preliminaries

Before you begin, sketch a rough draft of your stepping stone design. If you plan on making a series of mosaic stepping stones, you'll want to plan where you'll place the tiles before setting tiles in stone. (Excuse the pun!) You can mix and match decorative materials, create unadorned colored stones, or create a blueprint so each stone looks the same. The choice is yours. Have fun with it!

Supplies

- **Cement mix**
- **Mixing trough or wheelbarrow**
- **Hoe**
- **Concrete sealant**
- **Rubber gloves**
- **Spray cooking oil**
- **Cement trowel or a 2 x 4 wood scrap for leveling**
- **Cake pans or other mold**
- **Decorative elements**
- **Sturdy scissors**
- **Sandpaper**

Steps

1. Follow directions on concrete package and mix ingredients in a wheelbarrow or mixing trough, using a hoe. Be sure to wear gloves, and take care not to splatter cement on bare skin.

2. Coat the inside of the molds with cooking oil.

3. Fill cake pans to the top with concrete. If pans are especially deep, fill pan 1½" (3.8 cm) deep. To remove air bubbles tap mold on the ground. Level the top to create a smooth surface for creative play.

4. Wait for concrete to set slightly before pushing decorative items into the surface. There is no exact rule on timing, but be sure concrete is fairly stable before placing heavy stones into the mold. Use cookie cutters to make shapes, and write messages with popsicle sticks. Or, rely on a cookie cutter alphabet.

5. Allow stones to dry according to directions on the cement package. Ease stepping stones out of the mold, or cut away the disposable pan. Use sandpaper to smooth any rough edges.

6. Finally, apply a coat of sealant to weatherproof your design.

PROJECT PAIRINGS

FIND A PLACE for your homemade stepping stones with these projects:

Install Bed Edging

Bed edging outlines and divides distinct landscape features, usually separating plant beds from turf. Edging holds together the intricate patchwork of color and texture in a bed and defines a space as special. It also prevents creeping plants from overstepping their boundaries and flowing into turf areas. Edging serves as a barrier that contains mulch and soil in beds, and it prevents turf roots from invading planting areas.

Besides these functional benefits, there are aesthetic reasons to finish your work with edging. A basic border will confine an island of plants in a sea of green turf or define an existing bed situated on the perimeter of your property. Edging is neat and clean. And you can accomplish this cost-effective finishing touch in just hours.

FRAME YOUR LANDSCAPE with bed edging. You can choose among a variety of materials, from wood to decorative stone.

The Dirt

Get inspired by the array of edging materials, from stone, brick, and metal to recycled-plastic products, which are a weather-friendly alternative to wood. We'll show you how to install the standard, black plastic edging commonly found in garden supply stores. This option is convenient because it conforms to curved or straight edges, and it is relatively inexpensive.

Preliminaries

Time this project when soil is moist, not parched after a drought period or sopping from a week of rain. Driving stakes into the soil to secure bed edging is much easier when the ground is soft.

Before beginning a bed edging project, take care to do the following:

- **Be sure** the bed is located where you want it. If you choose to redesign the size or shape, do this before digging the trench for the edging.
- **Measure** the perimeter of the bed. Then measure it again. Accuracy will help you avoid repeat trips to the garden supply store.
- **Choose** edging material based on your style, the bed's shape and size, and its plantings.
- **Ensure** that the ground is soft so you can easily dig a trench and drive in stability stakes.

Supplies

- **4" (10.2 cm) edging**
- **Edging connectors and corners**
- **Spade**
- **Hand maul**
- **Edging stakes**
- **Utility knife**

Steps

1. Carefully measure the perimeter of the bed and purchase edging.

2. Unroll the edging in the sun and allow it to warm up. The edging is easier to work with when it is warm.

Figure 1

3. Prepare a trench along the bed edge by cutting straight down on the turf side, using a spade. Angle the trench into the bed to allow room for driving in stakes.

4. Place the edging in the trench so the base of the round top is at ground level and the edging is aligned vertically. Drive a stake partially through the bed-side point of the edging to secure it **(Figure 1)**.

5. Continue placing the edging and driving stakes. Use connectors to splice pieces together for long runs. Cut the edging to size with a utility knife. To create sharp corners, purchase right angle edging connectors.

6. When you are satisfied with the edging placement, drive the stakes in completely. Fill the trench with soil, and press soil into any gaps on the turf side of the edging.

PROJECT PAIRINGS

NOW THAT YOU'VE DEFINED a planting space with a border, try these inventive planting techniques:

Lath Trellis

A simple trellis serves as an ideal support for climbing plants. Because foliage and blooms are the centerpiece, your structure should act as a skeleton, providing the framework to encourage interesting, vertical growth. Trellises add a cottage feel to a landscape design, and they can be used as dividers to create "rooms" in a garden. Or, placed against a home or wall, trellises serve as leaning ladders on which ivy can climb.

This is an excellent beginner construction project because the parts are simple to cut and construct. We'll provide a plan for a trellis here, but you can adapt it by playing with various arrangements for the trim.

The Dirt

A trellis is an aesthetic feature, but it must be functional. It should accommodate the space where you want to place it and the plants it will support. So think first, where will you place the trellis? What is the growing habit of the vines that will climb the structure? Fast growers may need a taller trellis. Also keep in mind surrounding elements: fences, gates, trees, tall shrubs, and walls. Your trellis should be of similar proportion. Think how ridiculous a 5-foot (1.5 m) trellis would look up against a 9-foot (2.7 m) fence!

Next, consider design elements. Vertical legs help your trellis stand, and you should incorporate an odd number of legs for interest. (We use five legs in this project.) This odd rule is a principle in flower arranging, as well. One is dramatic, two looks weak. Three is interesting, four is just missing something. The fifth, and so on. Think odd numbers, and stagger the heights of vertical legs. Make every other one 3 inches (7.6 cm) taller or more for a rustic effect.

Finally, you can experiment with motif as you arrange the trellis trim in patterns, such as diamonds. You can mimic existing themes in your garden. And don't forget the paint! Blend trellises with the background with earthy browns or greens, or choose a contrast color to add drama. White is conservative and clean, but a series of trellises in bright colors is fun and whimsical.

Preliminaries

Before you begin, sketch your trellis to scale. Each vertical leg for this project is ¾ inch (1.9 cm) wide. You should place vertical legs 4 to 8 inches (10.2 to 20.3 cm) apart. (We allowed 6 inches [15.2 cm]) You can follow our plan, or measure your space and use this guide to create your own recipe. Also, you will attach at least three horizontal supports across the legs: one at the bottom, another two-thirds from the bottom, and a third about 2 inches (5.1 cm) from the top of the trellis. You can add more horizontal supports if necessary.

Figure 1

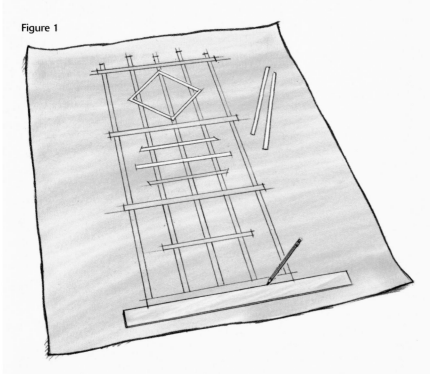

Design: To experiment with design, draw a full-size pattern of your trellis on kraft paper, which is large enough to accommodate a life-sized sketch. Cut ¾-inch (1.9-cm) strips of paper that will serve as experimental trim. Now, play with various designs by rearranging the strips on the drawing of your trellis base **(Figure 1)**.

Cutting: Use these strips as a pattern for cutting trim pieces from screen moldings. Tape the pattern to the wood and make the cuts. A back saw and miter box will make it easier to make clean angled cuts. Cut the remaining pieces to size based on your design. Use the parting stop for the vertical legs. Cut the lath equal to the finished width of the trellis for the horizontal supports. Cut another set of horizontal supports from the lath that are 2 inches (5.1 cm) longer.

Supplies
- **Drill**
- **Saw**
- **Wire cutters**
- **½" x ¾" (1.3 x 1.9 cm) pine parting stop**
- **¼" x 1⅜" (0.7 x 3.4 cm) pine lath**
- **¼" x ¾" (0.7 x 1.9 cm) pine or oak screen moldings**
- **Exterior wood glue**
- **½" (13 mm) wire brads**
- **Exterior primer and paint**
- **#3 rebar for mounting**

Steps

1. Place vertical legs flat on the ground 6" (15.2 cm) apart. Glue and nail the shorter horizontal supports to the legs. Secure the supports with two brads at each joint. Flip over the trellis. Following the same technique, secure the longer pieces of horizontal lath by lining them up against the horizontal supports. This lath extends 1" (2.5 cm) beyond the trellis on either side.

2. Place the screen molding onto the trellis based on your design. Apply glue to joints. Drill pilot holes, and drive brads into place where molding intersects legs. Place a scrap of lath under the trellis for support.

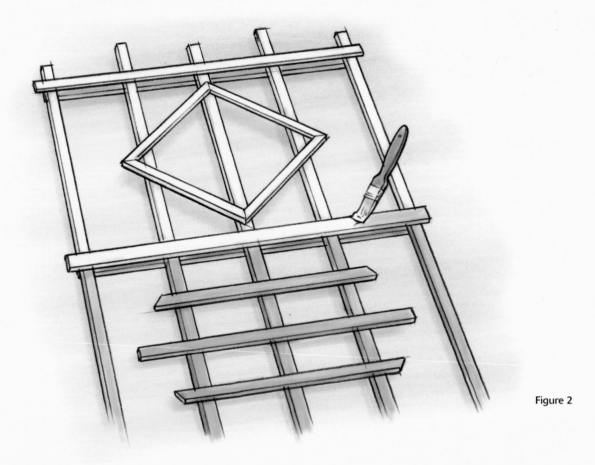

Figure 2

3. Paint as desired **(Figure 2)**.

4. You can use a surface or freestanding mount to secure your trellis in the desired location.

    Surface mount: Stack and glue three 6" (15.2 cm) pieces of lath together. After the glue dries, cut the stack into four 1⅜" (3.5 cm) squares. Drill pilot holes through the outer top leg and horizontal support joints. Place a square between the trellis and the wall or fence and drive a galvanized deck screw through the joint, the square, and into the wall. Repeat for the other upper corner, then for the lower outer corners.

    Freestanding mount: Drive two pieces of #3 rebar into the ground at each end of trellis. Using plastic-coated wire, secure trellis to the stakes at several points on each side, working your way up to the top. Be sure the stakes are buried at least 12" (30.5 cm) into the ground and extend above ground at least half the height of the trellis.

PROJECT PAIRINGS

TRY THESE complementary projects:

PROJECT

Build an Arbor

Arbors add romance to a landscape as a dramatic entrance to a patio or garden space. A row of arbors with rounded tops forms a tunnel passageway from one outdoor room to the next, while a single arbor teeming with climbing roses or clematis serves as a whimsical entrance to a cottage garden. Arched arbors are a traditional outdoor wedding backdrop. But the structure takes on many shapes, such as the basic, square arbor post-and-beam arbor you'll create in this project. In a sense, the arbor is the front porch of the landscape: a warm welcome to visit and take in the setting beyond its frame.

The Dirt

You can compose an arbor from an assortment of materials, ranging from branches or latticework covered with climbing shrubs or vines to formal Greek columns. This sturdy arbor made of cedar is a post-and-slat structure that is solid yet airy.

Add lattice or a trellis as sides to the arbor for more privacy. You can encourage vine growth on this cedar arbor by attaching screw eyes along the vertical posts and stringing wire between the eyes. Then, plant one climbing vine at the base of each post. Wisteria and clematis are happy climbers. As they grow, train them along the wires.

Preliminaries

You can adapt the size of this structure your space by adding more posts. Be sure that you do not place posts farther than 8 feet (2.4 m) apart. Doing so compromises the strength of the arbor.

Before breaking ground, used stakes to lay out the desired posthole locations. Tap four stakes into the ground at the desired location, measuring to be sure they are 60 inches (152 cm) apart. To check measurements for accuracy, measure across the diagonals. These measurements should be equal if you have laid out a true square. Align two additional stakes beyond each posthole stake. Then, tie string around each post, forming a square **(Figure 1)**.

2 x 2
cross strip

2 x 6
tie beam

2 x 4
rafters

cement

4 x 4 post

gravel

ARBORS CAN RESEMBLE arched trellises, such as the one pictured. or take on a more solid structure.

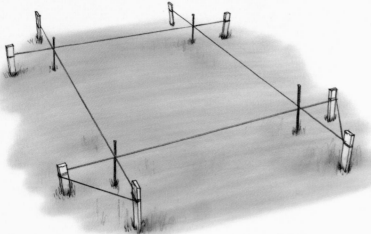

Figure 1

Supplies

- **Stakes and string**
- **Tape measure**
- **Hammer**
- **Posthole digger or power auger**
- **Shovel**
- **Wheelbarrow**
- **Concrete mix**
- **Hoe**
- **Gravel**
- **Power drill**
- **Level**
- **Line level**
- **Reciprocating saw**
- **Clamps**
- **10-foot (3m) 4 x 4 posts (305 x 8.9 x 8.9 cm) (4)**
- **7' (2.1m) 2 x 6 tie beams (213 x 3.8 x 14 cm) (2)**
- **7' (2.1m) 2 x 4 rafters (213 x 3.8 x 8.9 cm) (4)**
- **7' (2.1m) 2 x 2 cross strips (213 x 3.8 x 3.8 cm) (7)**
- **Nonstaining 2¼" (57 mm) deck screws**
- **3" (76 mm) lag screws (8)**
- **Rafter ties and nails (8)**
- **Wood sealer**
- **Paintbrush**

Steps

1. Remove the string from the stakes and remove the stakes marking the postholes. Using the posthole digger, dig holes to required depth (refer to building code). Place 6" (15.2 cm) of gravel in the bottom of each hole.

2. Set posts in the holes. Restring the string around the second set of stakes to mark the post placements. Align the posts, check the posts for level and brace them upright. To brace, screw support boards to the posts on adjoining faces. Drive stakes into the ground so they are flush against each brace. Drive galvanized deck screws through the stakes into the braces. **(Figure 2)**.

3. Mix concrete in the wheelbarrow for one post at a time, according to instruction on the bag. Pour concrete into postholes, and check posts for plumb immediately before concrete sets. Wait 24 hours for concrete to dry.

4. Install tie beams. Measure, mark, and cut lumber for the arbor as such:

- Cut a 3" x 3" (7.6 x 6.7 cm) notch off the bottom corners of each tie beam.
- Cut a 2" x 2" (5.1 x 5.1 cm) notch off the bottom corner of each rafter.
- Cut a 1" x 1" (2.5 x 2.5 cm) notch off the bottom corner of each cross strip.

Figure 2

Check your local building code for footing depth requirements and setback restrictions before you dig postholes.

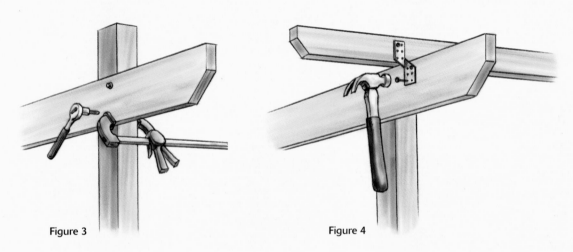

Figure 3

Figure 4

5. Position a tie beam against the outside edge of a pair of posts, 7 feet (2.1 m) above the ground and clamp in place. The beam should extend 1 foot (30 cm) past the post on each side to form an overhang.

6. Level the beam. Drill two ⅜" (9.5 mm) pilot holes through the tie beam and into each post. Attach the tie beam to the posts with 3" (76 mm) lag screws **(Figure 3)**.

7. Use a line level to mark the opposite pair of posts at the same height as the first tie beam. Repeat the process in steps 5 and 6 to attach the second beam.

8. Cut off posts so they are level with the tops of the tie beams. A reciprocating saw or handsaw will do the job.

9. Attach rafters using rafter ties and galvanized nails. Rafters are spaced 24" (60.9 cm) apart, beginning 6" (15.2 cm) from the ends of the tie beams. Ends will extend past each tie beam by 12" (30.5 cm) to form the overhang **(Figure 4)**.

10. Install cross strips by positioning them across the top of rafters, spacing them 12" (30.5 cm) apart, beginning 6" (15.2 cm) from the ends of the rafters **(Figure 5)**. Drill pilot

holes through the cross strip and into the rafters. Attach the cross strip with nonstaining deck screws. Add remaining cross strips.

11. Apply wood sealer or paint, as desired.

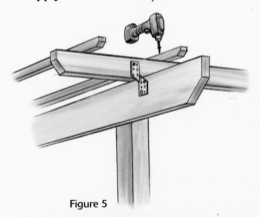

Figure 5

PROJECT PAIRINGS

WITH AN ARBOR in place, these projects are a natural fit:

Lath Trellis	**130**
Create airy walls for your arbor.	
Garden Benches	**140**
Create a seating area to enjoy your arbor space.	
Dining al Fresco	**204**
Now that you're under cover, incorporate these design features for outdoor entertainment.	

Perfect Pergola

A PERGOLA EXTENDS from a home and forms
an airy roof for patio spaces.

As you design your outdoor living room,
consider what qualities define a space as comfortable,
relaxing, and protected. Shelter is the most obvious
distinction between a dining room and backyard patio.
A pergola serves this purpose and more. It is a safe haven

in a garden, providing a light, airy, inviting space for people to gather. We'll show you how to make one in this project, and you can adjust the size to your liking by simply adding more posts and rafters to extend the length.

The Dirt

Pergolas are close cousins to arbors, and can be freestanding or attached to a structure, such as your home. You can dress up pergolas by hanging planters from the rafters, or add outdoor holiday lights to the structure for special occasions or anytime, really. You can stream weather-ready fabrics through pergola rafters for a soft, flowing effect, which will also create more of a cover from the elements. Get creative! A pergola is a structure designed for embellishment. Or, allow the simple beauty of unadorned cedar wood to blend with the surroundings.

Preliminaries

The basic instructions for building an arbor apply to this project. Here, we convert the arbor project to a pergola by increasing the dimensions of the project, therefore extending the cover to more of a roof than an entryway. Review instructions in Build an Arbor on page 134. The arbor project provides technique for digging postholes, installing tie beams, and attaching rafters and cross strips.

This pergola measures 10 feet by 5 feet (3 m by 1.5 m), double the length of the arbor. You can increase the length and width of your pergola based on your space, but do not spread the vertical beams farther than 8 feet (2.4 m) apart.

Supplies

- **Refer to Build an Arbor (page 134) for tools**
- **10' 4 x 4 posts (305 x 8.9 x 8.9 cm) (6)**
- **7' 2 x 6 tie beams (213 x 3.8 x 14 cm) (3)**
- **12' 2 x 4 rafters (366 x 3.8 x 8.9 cm) (8)**
- **7' 2 x 2 cross strips (213 x 3.8 x 3.8 cm) (12)**
- **Non staining 2¼" (57 mm) deck screws**
- **3" (76 mm) lag screws (12)**
- **Rafter ties and nails (12)**

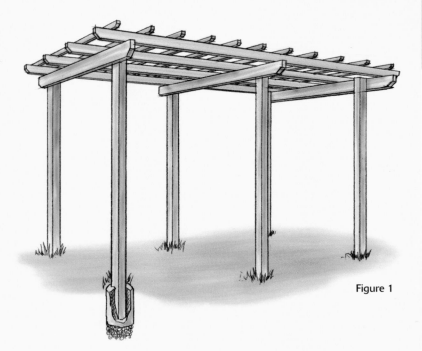

Figure 1

Steps

1. Refer to Build an Arbor Steps, working through building technique and adding extra pergola pieces when necessary. For this project, dig six postholes and attach three tie beams. The rafter and cross strip spacing remains the same **(Figure 1)**.

2. Paint your pergola, or finish with a wood sealant.

3. Decorate your pergola with colorful fabrics, lights, or hanging plants.

PROJECT PAIRINGS

TRY THESE PROJECTS to dress up your pergola:

Container Planting Clinic   104
The same rules to container plantings apply to hanging baskets, which make great ornaments for pergola rafters.

Lath Trellis   130
Add walls to your pergola.

Build an Arbor   134
You can build off your structural theme by creating an arbor in another are of your landscape.

PROJECT

Garden Benches

If you take on even a portion of the projects in this book, you deserve a place to unwind and enjoy the fruits of your labor. So much of our time in the yard is dedicated to doting over flowers, maintaining lawns, and caring for trees and shrubs. With our hands in the garden and our minds focused on what's next to improve the landscape, we spend a great deal of our time on our hands and knees, getting the job done. Now, it's about time you enjoy the features you designed and installed.

What better way to celebrate your two green thumbs than to rest easy on a garden bench? Pay attention to this seat as you would any landscape element. Its placement should be intentional; temporary seating is easily fulfilled by plastic lawn chairs. This is *your* spot. We'll show you how to make it sturdy and classic-looking so it meshes with most any style.

The Dirt

Time to get inspired. Where will you place your bench? The location of your seating area will allow you, or any visitor who perches there, to enjoy a fresh perspective of your landscape. Consider spaces that appeal to the senses. This could mean a plot far away from high-traffic areas of your property, so you can meditate and enjoy the outdoors.

While considering the ideal spot for your bench, factor in the land grade. You should choose an area that is level. Otherwise, plan on compensating for uneven ground by propping up bench legs or preparing the ground by filling in ruts and other imperfections.

This particular wood bench can be painted or stained to blend with surroundings. However, you may opt for a prefabricated bench that you can purchase at a garden store. You'll find a selection that ranges in material from metals to plastics. Before you buy, decide whether your bench will be a permanent fixture in your yard or if you

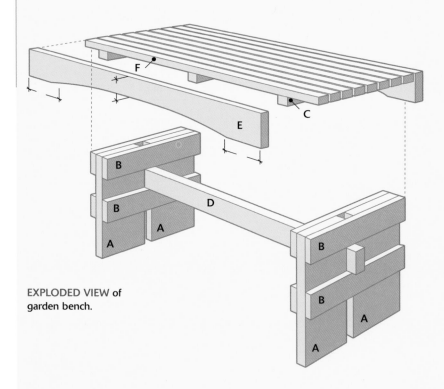

EXPLODED VIEW of garden bench.

Cutting List

KEY	PART	DIMENSION INCHES (CM)	PCS.
A	Leg half	1½ x 7¼ x 14½ (3.8 x 18.5 x 36.8)	4
B	Cleat	¾ x 3½ x 16 (1.9 x 8.9 x 40.6)	8
C	Brace	1½ x 1½ x 16 (3.8 x 3.8 x40.6)	3
D	Trestle	1½ x 3½ x 60 (3.8 x 8.9 x 152.4)	1
E	Apron	1½ x 5½ x 60 (3.8 x 14 x 152.4)	2
F	Slat	1½ x1½ x 60 (3.8 x 3.8 x 152.4)	8

will move it indoors in bad weather. Properly treated, the bench in this project lends itself to four-season use.

Preliminaries

This project requires equipment you may not have at home. You can rent a circular saw from a hardware store. As with any power equipment, practice precaution by wearing eye protection, jeans to cover legs, and closed-toe shoes in case you fumble during the construction process.

A reminder about measurements: Your care as you build will pay off with a sturdy bench. Cut corners and you may wind up with a trick chair that dumps you flat.

Supplies

- **Circular saw**
- **Drill**
- **Tape measure**
- **Hammer**
- **Sandpaper**
- **1½-inch (38 mm) deck screws**
- **2½-inch (64 mm) deck screws**
- **Exterior wood glue**
- **Casing nails (3)**
- **Wood sealer/stain**
- **8-foot 2 x 2 cedar (243.8 x 3.8 x 3.8 cm) (6)**
- **6-foot 2 x 8 cedar (182.9 x 3.8 x 19 cm) (1)**
- **6-foot 1 x 4 cedar (182.9 x 1.9 x 8.9 cm) (2)**
- **6-foot 2 x 4 cedar (182.9 x 3.8 x 8.9 cm) (1)**
- **6-foot 2 x 6 cedar (182.9 x 3.8 x 14 cm (2)**

Steps

1. Cut cedar wood according to the dimensions in the cutting list.

2. Place one leg half between two top cleats so cleats are flush with the top and outside edge of the leg half. Join the parts by driving four 1½" (38 mm) deck screws through each cleat and into the leg half. Repeat the process for the remaining two cleats and leg half.

3. Stand these two assemblies upright with the open ends of the cleat pointing upward, about 4 feet (121 cm) apart. Place the trestle onto leg halves, so it forms a letter I. The trestle should hang 1½" (3.8 cm) past each side. Fasten the trestle with glue, then secure with 2½" (64 mm) deck screws **(Figure 1)**.

4. Slide the other leg half between the cleats, keeping the edges flush and join using glue and 2½" (38 mm) deck screws. Attach the two bottom cleats snug against the bottom of the trestle. Use glue and 1½" (38 mm) deck screws. Repeat for the other bench side.

5. Fasten a brace to the inner top cleat on each side so tops are flush.

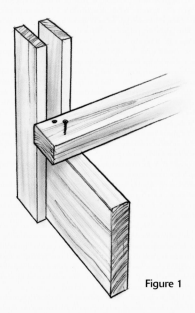

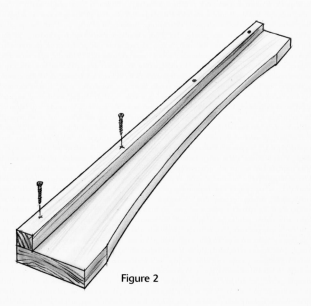

Figure 1

Figure 2

6. Create the arch in the aprons. Drive a casing nail slightly into the apron 3" (7.6 cm) in from each end along a long side. Drive the third nail at the midpoint of the apron, 1½" (3.8 cm) up from the side. Arch a flexible metal ruler between the nails. Trace the arch with a pencil and cut out with a jigsaw. Attach the end slats to the top inside edge of each apron, using wood glue and deck screws **(Figure 2)**.

7. Place the apron-slat assemblies upside down. Flip the leg and trestle assembly so it is face down on top of the slats and between the aprons. The aprons will extend 1½" (3.8 cm) beyond the legs at each end of the bench. Drive 2½" (64 mm) deck screws through the braces into both slats.

8. Place the remaining brace between aprons, centered. Attach with glue and 2½" (64 mm) deck screws.

9. Position the six remaining slats under the braces, using ½" (1.3 cm) spacers to create equal gaps between each slat. Attach slats with glue and drive deck screws through braces into each slat **(Figure 3)**.

10. Sand the bench. Finish with exterior paint, a clear wood sealer, or stain of your choice.

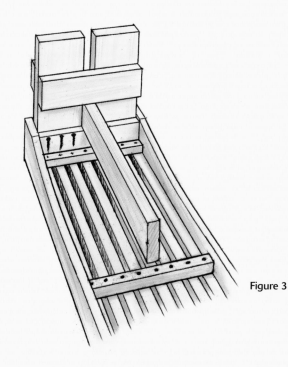

Figure 3

PROJECT PAIRINGS

YOU'VE CREATED a resting place to enjoy these projects:

PROJECT

Tree Stump Solutions

BREATHE NEW LIFE into an old stump by converting it into a useful planter.

Stumped about what to do with the remains of an old oak or any sizeable tree that now exists as a peg leg of its former self? The fact is, tree stump removal is a messy process that requires replanting the area, and there are plenty of alternatives that allow you to reinvent the eyesore into a landscape feature. A tree stump serves as an ideal raised planter. Surround it with a group of potted flowers, and the rustic "container" will stand out as a unique focal point. In this project, we'll show how to create a quirky planter from a stump.

Large tree stumps radiate heat as they decompose. For plants, this means a warm, fertile environment.

The Dirt

A tree stump is a great foundation for numerous projects. Why build a bench if you can transform a tree stump into a stool? Use a chainsaw to cut the stump to the appropriate height, chisel a design into a chair back if desired, and sand the chair to prevent splinters. Apply a coat of weather-resistant polyurethane, and you're set. Add a patio umbrella to the area to shade your resting spot, or surround it with plants.

What about the birds who nested in its canopy? You can reinvent their home by placing an attractive birdhouse in the center of the stump as a display. If the stump is hollow, encourage vine growth up a trellis (*see Vines for Landscapes, page 86*) to disguise the stump and provide a protected place for birds, who look for natural nooks and crannies to call home.

Preliminaries

Naturally, your stump must be hollow to function as a planter. You can chisel and grind out the stump yourself. This is a laborious task, so consider asking the tree service to manage this for you as they remove the tree.

The steps to plant and prepare the soil for a tree stump planter are the same as those in Container Planting Clinic (page 104). You'll use a similar design concept, working in layers of plants. Especially important for a stump planter is incorporating trailing varieties that disguise the stump.

Supplies

- **Soil**
- **Plants**
- **Planting supplies** (page 31)
- **Stump grinder**
- **Drill and large spade bit**
- **Chisel**

Steps

1. Rent a stump grinder to remove the core of the stump, or hire a professional to do so. You also can use a drill and chisel to form a hole in the trunk, which will serve as your planter.

Stump Planter

2. Prepare the core of the stump as though it is a planter. Fill the stump with quality potting soil, stopping several inches (about 7.5 cm) from the top of the container.

3. Add plants, spacing them apart to allow for growth as they mature. Because each plant has different growth habits, do your homework, read plant tags, and ask questions of nursery professionals, who can steer you toward plants that will live well together. (*See recommendations in Container Planting Clinic, page 104.*)

4. Add more soil, until it reaches about 2" (5.1 cm) from the top of the container. Gently pat down soil.

PROJECT PAIRINGS

Cool, Creative Planters	110
Discover other interesting planter ideas.	
Ivy Topiary	112
A tree stump is a natural foundation for growing climbers.	
Garden Benches	140
If you turn your stump into a table, create a bench and belly up.	

Build a Birdhouse

Birds provide great entertainment, an impromptu show with a cast of winged characters. Learning about different species that visit your backyard, and sharing this curiosity with children, is a great outdoor education. So why not build a happy home for your feathered friends?

Here, we'll show you how to use basic hand tools and a simple construction technique. You can choose whether to coat the birdhouse in color or allow it to weather if you want it to blend with nature. Invite the children to help out with this project!

The Dirt

Colorful, whimsical birdhouses add punch and personality to garden areas, but bright paint is more pleasing to the human eye than to birds. If your goals is to attract nature's aviators, a less ostentatious finish will appeal to females, who generally avoid drawing attention to their nesting areas.

When choosing paint, buy exterior latex finish. Do not paint the interior; birds won't nest in a house that smells like humans. Dark colors absorb and retain heat, and birds prefer a cool abode. So choose lighter, duller colors, as opposed to high-gloss brights, if bird attraction is your goal.

If you don't want to paint your birdhouse, use cedar, redwood, or cypress. These materials are naturally rot resistant and do not require finish. These woods will naturally weather and turn gray as they age.

Finally, the size of your birdhouse will invite certain species to nest. (*See Main Attraction on page 148.*) Cut the entrance hole, which is the door to your birdhouse, exactly to specifications. Any larger and you could invite predators.

Preliminaries

Before you measure and cut wood, draw a plan for your birdhouse on paper. You can refer to this map during construction. Exact measurements are important with this and any project. Sloppy corners and lines result in awkward pieces that don't fit together, so pay attention to detail. A try square will help you draw perfect corners. Also, note instructions to mark centers and sides of each piece. These guides will help you assemble the birdhouse properly.

Power tools will reduce the labor for this project, but because you're building a *bird-house*, not a four-bedroom ranch, handsaws are safer to use with children and are appropriate for a project of this scope.

Supplies

- **4-foot 1 x 6 cedar (121.9 x 1.9 x 14cm) (1)**
- **4d (38 mm) galvanized finish nails**
- **Saw**
- **Hammer**
- **Drill and bits**
- **1½ inch spade bit**
- **Tape measure**
- **Try square**
- **Paintbrush**
- **Exterior wood glue**
- **Shoulder hook**
- **Sandpaper**
- **Exterior latex paint (optional)**

Cutting List

KEY	PART	SIZE INCHES (CM)	PCS.
A	Side	1 x 4 x 5½ (2.5 x 10.2 x 14)	2
B	Roof	1 x 5½ x 6½ (2.5 x 14 x 16.5)	1
C	Roof	1 x 4¾ x 6½ (2.5 x 12 x 16.5)	1
D	Front/Back	1 x 5½ x 8¾ (2.5 x 14 x 10.8)	2
E	Bottom	1 x 4 x 4 (1.5 x 10.2 x 10.2)	1

Steps

1. Cut the birdhouse parts to size following the cutting list.

2. Mark each side of front and back pieces 2¾" (5.75 cm) from the top. Mark the center point at the top. Mark lines from the center point to each side, then cut along them to form the roof peak.

3. On the bottom piece, make a diagonal cut across each corner ½" (1.3 cm) from the end to allow for drainage.

4. Mark a point on the front piece 2" (5.1 cm) down from the peak, centering the mark from side to side. Use a spade bit to drill an entrance hole about 1½" (3.8 cm) in diameter. Hole size will vary depending on the type of bird you want to attract. *(See Main Attraction on page 148.)*

5. Use a wood screw to make several deep horizontal scratches on the inside of the front piece, below the entrance hole. These grip lines help young birds hold on as they climb up to the entrance hole.

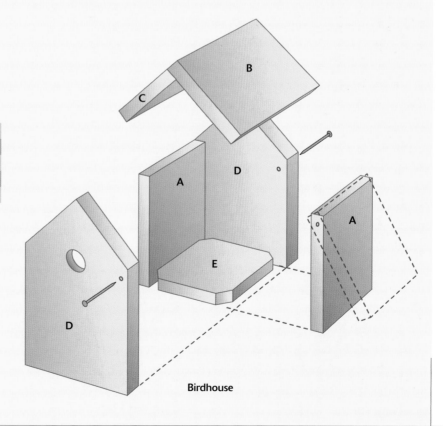

Birdhouse

Always wear safety glasses when using saws of any kind. Also, review safety tips with children, and stress that tools are helpful, but potentially dangerous.

6. Apply wood glue to one edge of the bottom piece so bottoms of two pieces are flush.

7. Drill $\frac{1}{16}$ inch (1 mm) pilot holes and attach pieces using 4d (38 mm) galvanized finish nails. Repeat this process for the front and back pieces, aligning edges with the side piece.

8. Set the remaining side piece in place, but don't glue it. To attach the side to the front and back pieces, drive a 4d (38 mm) nail through the front wall and another through the back wall, each positioned about ⅝" (1.6 cm) from the top edge. This arrangement allows the piece to pivot.

9. Apply glue to top edges of one side of the front and back pieces. Set the smaller roof piece on the house so its upper edge is aligned with the peak of the house. Apply glue to the top edges on the opposite side of the front and back pieces. Place the larger roof piece in position. Drill pilot holes and drive 4d nails through the roof into the front piece and then the back.

10. Drill a pilot hole in the edge of the front piece on the pivot wall side, placed about 1 inch (2.5 cm) from the bottom edge of the house. Screw in a shoulder hook, positioning it to hold the side piece closed.

11. Sand the birdhouse smooth, then paint or decorate it as desired.

MAIN ATTRACTION

Bird species prefer different-sized homes. Depending on what you want to attract to your birdhouse, you can adapt your construction measurements as follows:

BIRD	FLOOR Inches (cm)	DEPTH Inches (cm)	HOLE SIZE Inches (cm)	HEIGHT OF HOLE FROM FLOOR Inches (cm)
Barn swallow	6 x 6 (15.2x15.2)	6 (15.2)	one side open	
Bluebird	5 x 5 (12.7x12.7)	8 (20.3)	1½ (3.8)	6 (15.2)
Chickadee	4 x 4 (10.2x10.2)	8–10 (20.3–25.4)	1⅛ (2.7)	6–8 (15.2–20.3)
House wren	4 x 4 (10.2x10.2))	6–8 15.2–20.3)	1–1¼ (2.5-3.1)	4–6 (10.2–15.2)
Redheaded woodpecker	6 x 6 (15.2x15.2)	12–15 (30.5–38.1)	2 (5.1)	9–12 (22.9–30.5)
Robin	6 x 8 (15.2x20.3)	8 (20.3)	one side open	
Screech Owl	8 x 8 (20.3x20.3)	12–15 (30.5–38.1)	3 (7.6)	9–12 (22.9–30.5)

ONCE YOU'VE MASTERED the basic skills of birdhouse building, be adventurous and try alternative materials and styles.

Interlock Retaining Wall

Steep slopes are harbingers of erosion and drainage problems. Keeping turf alive on a severe grade is always a challenge, so a hillside evolves into a problem area over time. Retaining walls are a solution. By carving steps out of a slope and inserting an aesthetically pleasing wall, you form a shelf of usable space where you can plant flowers. Meanwhile, for properties that lack depth, retaining walls create layers. You can actually build a split-level backyard where a patio space overlooks the landscape, or vice-versa.

The Dirt

Whether your reason for a retaining wall is for functional or purely aesthetic purposes, the process is simplified with interlocking block. It doesn't require mortar, and you can find it in various styles and colors that complement your home or landscape features. These formed concrete blocks are level on top, eliminating the challenge of finding rocks with like surfaces. As long as your trench is level and you take care to measure the site before installing the block, you'll achieve an even, professional finish.

Preliminaries

If your retaining wall will exceed 4 feet (1.2 m) in height, call a professional to assist with the job. The higher the wall, the more pressure it must withstand from the soil and water behind it—thousands of pounds. Significant walls also require building permits and special techniques, including an engineered design.

CREATE SHELVES for plantings and add tiers of interest to your backyard with a retaining wall.

Supplies

- **Plate compactor**
- **Shovel**
- **Trenching spade**
- **Wheelbarrow**
- **Stakes**
- **String**
- **Line level**
- **Level**
- **Landscape fabric**
- **Compactible gravel**
- **Interlocking block and capstones**
- **Perforated drain tile**
- **Hand tamp**
- **Concrete adhesive**
- **Caulk gun**

Steps

1. Excavate the slope, creating a level area for the wall. Allow at least 1 foot (0.3 m) between the back of the wall and slope for gravel backfill **(Figure 1)**.

2. Insert stakes to mark the ends of the wall, and all curves and corners. Connect stakes with string, and check the string with a line level, making necessary adjustments.

3. Dig a trench for the first row of block. Dig 8 inches (20.3 cm) deeper than the height of the block. (If the block is 4 inches [10.2 cm] tall, dig a 12 inch [30.5-cm] trench.) Measure the trench along the string outline to ensure it is even in all areas. This will serve as the foundation for your wall, and you want it to be completely level.

4. Cut landscape fabric for lining the excavated area. Allow 3 feet (0.9 m) of excess fabric to extend past the top of the wall, onto the shelf you will create. Overlap strips by 6 inches (15.2 cm) as you lay them down.

5. Spread 6 inches (15.2 cm) of compactable gravel into the trench. Use a plate compactor to press it into the trench.

6. Lay the first row of blocks into the trench, aligning front edges with string. If blocks have flanged or shaped surfaces, install the first row backwards so the smooth surface faces forward. While installing blocks, use a level to check for evenness.

7. Lay the second row of blocks, staggering the joints in a running block pattern.

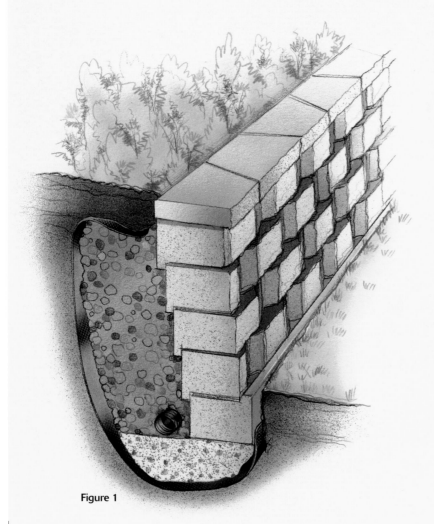

Figure 1

If your slope exceeds 4 feet (1.2 m) in height, you can create a terrace effect with a series of retaining walls. Build the first retaining wall, then progress up the slope and build the next, allowing several feet between layers. The bleacher effect will provide shelves for plantings and reduce erosion problems.

8. Add 1 to 2 inches (2.5 to 5.1 cm) of gravel, and place a perforated drain tile on top of the gravel, about 6 inches (15.2 cm) behind blocks. Perforations should face down. One end of the pipe should be unobstructed so runoff water can escape **(Figure 2)**.

9. Continue laying rows of block, paying attention to joints, until you have only capstones remaining.

10. Backfill the wall with coarse gravel, and pack it down with a hand tamp.

11. Fold the 3 feet (0.9 m) of landscape fabric over the gravel backfill. Add a thin layer of topsoil over fabric, and lightly pack down the soil with the hand tamp. (Fold excess fabric back over soil area, clearing the top row of block so you can install the capstones.)

12. Apply concrete adhesive to top blocks. Lay capstones in place **(Figure 3)**.

13. Fill topsoil behind the wall and in the trench at the base of the wall. Sod the area, or plant it as desired.

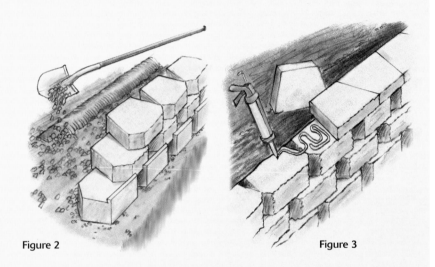

Figure 2   Figure 3

PROJECT PAIRINGS

TAKE YOUR SKILLS TO NEW HEIGHTS by exploring these options:

PROJECT

Brick Paver Patio

Brick is a timeless surface that suits most any style. It complements garden spaces, agrees with most home designs, and can be arranged in as many patterns as you can think to create from rectangles. Weathered, it takes on an old-world look. A neat-and-clean patterned brick patio provides a rhythmic focal point.

Consider this surface a canvas for features and accessories you incorporate into your outdoor living room, whether furniture or interesting planters. Because brick pavers are durable, you can expect them to withstand the elements and outlive even the hardiest perennials in your landscape. Here, we'll show you how to install concrete brick pavers, which are a user-friendly version of their clay counterparts.

The Dirt

Concrete pavers have self-spacing lugs, which automatically separate the bricks for joints. Press two brick pavers together, side by side, and the lugs will meet at the base, leaving a gap at the top of the paver. Compacted sand you apply as you finish the surface will create a firm seam. Sand is an easy material to work with when setting concrete brick pavers—if you don't like the position of the brick, you aren't literally stuck. A 1-inch (2.5-cm) sand base spread over a prepared gravel base serves as a foundation for pavers. Once pavers are put in place, sand is spread on the surface, and pressed into joints with a plate compactor. The result are sand seams that allow bricks to shift as temperatures change and the ground expands and contracts.

Preliminaries

Estimate the materials you will need for your space using the following equations:

Gravel (4 inch [10.2 cm] layer): surface area (square feet) divided by 50 = tons needed. (Cubic meters times 2.4 = metric tonnes needed.)

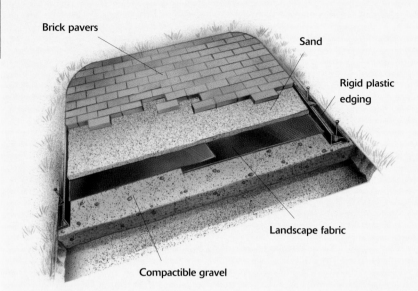

- Brick pavers
- Sand
- Rigid plastic edging
- Landscape fabric
- Compactible gravel

Figure 1

landscape fabric and lay them over the base, overlapping strips by at least 6 inches (15.2 cm). Anchor a strip of plastic edging into the perimeter by driving galvanized spikes through predrilled holes (in edging) and into the sub-base **(Figure 1)**. Now, you are ready to proceed with the brick paver project.

Supplies
- **Shovel**
- **Hand tamp**
- **Rubber mallet**
- **Carpenter's level**
- **2 x 4 lumber**
- **Circular saw with masonry blade**
- **Plate compactor**
- **Broom**
- **Landscape fabric**
- **Rigid plastic edging**
- **Galvanized spikes**
- **1" (2.5-cm) -thick pipe or wood strips**
- **Sand**
- **Brick pavers**

Steps
1. Lay 1 inch (2.5 cm) -thick pipes or wood strips over the landscape fabric, spaced every 6 feet (1.8 m). These are depth spacers for your sand base. Spread sand over the landscape fabric, smoothing it with a garden rake. Sand should just cover the top of spacers.

2. Water the layer of sand, then lightly pack it down with a hand tamp.

Sand: surface area (square feet) divided by 100 = tons needed (cubic meters times 1.6 = metric tonnes needed).

Brick pavers: surface area (square feet) times 5 = number of pavers needed

(surface area [square meters] times 45 = number of pavers needed)

Next, prepare the surface. If you are making a square or rectangular patio, use stakes and string to mark the area. Use a line level to determine whether strings are level. To check if an area is square or rectangular, measure across both diagonals. If the measurements are equal, the angles are correct. If your patio space is curved, use a rope or garden hose to define the border. To make even circles, make a large compass by tying a string to a stake and tying the string to a can of spray paint. Pull the string taut and spray the ground as you walk around the circle.

Now you are ready to excavate the area. Shovel out turf and dirt so the area 6 inches (15.2 cm) deeper than the thickness of the paver. You can place a 2 x 4 in the trenched area to determine if the ground is level. Next, pour compactible gravel into the area, and rake it into a smooth, 4 inch (10.2 cm) layer. Use a plate compactor to tamp the gravel into a firm surface.

A layer of landscape fabric on the gravel provides a smooth base for sand. Cut strips of

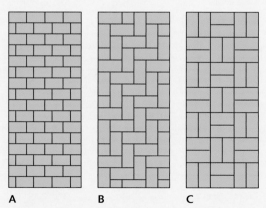

A   B   C

Figure 2

THREE COMMON BRICK arrangements are running bond (A), herring bone (B), and basketweave (C).

You can arrange rectangular pavers in various patterns (Figure 2). Also, brick pavers are available in a variety of colors, so look beyond the basic orange-brown color for options that may better suit your landscape.

Figure 3

Figure 4

3. Slide a straight 2 x 4 across the spacers to scrape away excess sand. Fill in any low spots.

4. Remove the spacers and fill in the grooves left behind. Compact with the hand tamp **(Figure 3)**.

5. Set the first section of pavers. Lay the first border paver in one corner, making sure it rests firmly against the plastic edging. Lay the next paver snug against the first. As you go along, set pavers by tapping them into the sand with a mallet. Refer to the depth of the first paver as a guide for the remaining pavers. Work in 2-foot (0.6-m) sections.

6. After setting each section, use a level to ensure that pavers are flat. Adjust uneven pavers by tapping them deeper into the sand or removing low pavers and adding a deeper sand cushion.

7. Install pavers in a fan pattern at rounded corners. Cut pavers to accommodate sharp bends **(Figure 4)**. Use a circular saw and masonry blade to accomplish this.

8. Continue laying 2-foot (0.6-m) sections of pavers, first working around the perimeter, then filling in the center of the area.

9. Spread a ½ inch (1.3 cm) layer of sand over the patio. Sweep the sand into the joints, then use the plate compactor to pack the sand tightly into the joints. Sweep away excess sand and soak the patio area with water. Repeat the process as necessary until joints are tightly packed.

PROJECT PAIRINGS

WITH A PATIO in place, take on these projects:

Seal Your Deck

After a deck weathers seasons of barbecues, snowstorms, foot traffic, and tree droppings, the surface will lose its fresh-wood crispness. Hard rain and those occasional airborne surprises, thanks to your deck being located under a bird migration pattern, will eat away the finish of a deck. Not pretty, is it?

Sealing a deck will add years to the structure's life. Think of sealant as an antiaging treatment, a face-lift of sorts. Cleaning and sealing your deck will restore its solid, smooth appearance—that is, if you do it properly. We'll show you how.

The Dirt

Not sure what type of sealer to use? There are many options on the market, and the temptation is to choose the "all-natural" sealer with oils. Keep in mind, these oils are food for algae and mildew, which will eat away deck sealer. If you opt for a natural sealer, select one that contains mildicides and algaecides. Meanwhile, synthetic sealer contains resins that don't appeal to mildew or algae. These are water-based and safe for the environment. Water-based, synthetic resin deck sealers are also available in a range of colors.

Preliminaries

Before you even open the can of sealer, the deck must be cleaned. This job can be quite a workout, and it does involve some elbow grease if you clean by hand. First clear the deck of debris, then clean the surface with an oxygen bleach/water mix. Some sealers can be applied immediately after cleaning, while the deck is still damp. Other products require a dry deck. Once you choose a sealer, carefully read instructions.

The right cleaning tools will make this job much easier. To apply the cleanser for soaking, you can use a hand-pump sprayer, similar to one you would use for liquid lawn treatments. Allow the liquid to sit on the deck for at least 15 minutes so the solution soaks in. This will make the job of scrubbing much easier. For scrubbing,

THINK OF YOUR DECK as hardwood floors in the great outdoors. Protect them with an annual cleaning and sealer.

hand-held plastic scrub brushes with nylon bristles are versatile, and you can purchase them at most grocery or hardware stores. A brush on a pole will save your back as you scrub the deck surface, and a toilet brush is ideal for wedging bristles into tight spaces, such as between rungs or underneath railings.

You can use a power washer to clean off the deck. This will get the job done faster, and you can rent or purchase this equipment from a home improvement store. However, we offer instructions on hand-scrubbing here because repeated power washing can wear away soft "spring" wood over time. Tim Carter, a nationally syndicated home improvement columnist and creator of Ask-TheBuilder.com, says power washers are ideal for many surfaces, but steer clear of using them on a deck. "Your deck will eventually look like a fishing pier," he relates.

For applying sealer, use a paintbrush, hand-pump sprayer and lambswool applicator. (These look like a

Oxygen bleach comes in a powder formula and is ideal for cleaning a deck. Do not use chlorine bleach, which is like arsenic to vegetation. It will kill plants, turf, and trees slowly over time.

scrub brush with a thick, fleece head rather than bristles.) Brushing on deck sealant is time-consuming, but necessary for areas like railings and hard-to-reach spaces. Otherwise, use a sprayer to apply sealer to deck boards, then smooth with a lambswool pad. This evens out the sealer.

Watch the clock with this project. Start the process in the morning or late afternoon, before temperatures climb past 75°F (24°C). That way, water and cleanser will evaporate more slowly.

Supplies
- **Water**
- **Powdered oxygen bleach**
- **Large bucket**
- **Hand-pump sprayer**
- **Cleaning brushes**
- **Deck sealer**
- **Paintbrush**
- **Lambswool applicator**

Steps

1. Remove all furniture and container plantings from deck and sweep the surface.

2. Mix 6 dry ounces powdered oxygen bleach per gallon of warm water (one part bleach to 21 parts water). Stir until completely dissolved. Apply cleaning solution to a small area, and scrub. Rinse the area thoroughly with clean water, then move on. Clean the deck first, then move on to railings and high areas.

3. Wait for the deck to dry completely before applying sealer. (Check instructions; water-based sealers can be brushed on damp surfaces.)

4. Apply sealer on railings and hard-to-reach areas with a paintbrush. Coat evenly. For more protection, apply two separate coats of

sealer rather than one thick layer. For larger surfaces, use a hand-spray tank to apply sealer to three deck boards at a time. Once you apply the sealer, follow up with a single swipe of the lambswool applicator. A smooth, continuous stroke will even out the sealer and allow just the right amount to soak into the deck **(Figure 1)**.

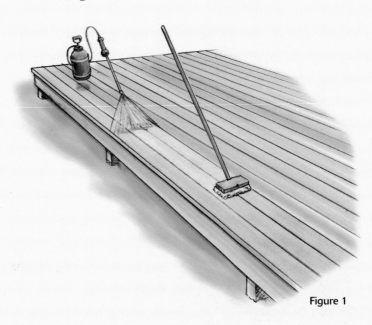

Figure 1

5. Allow the deck to dry thoroughly. Replace furniture, and fire up the grill. Time to enjoy!

PROJECT PAIRINGS

ENHANCE A DECK SPACE with these projects:

PROJECT

All about Awnings

Awnings, canopies, and sunroofs extend your patio season while adding character and color to your home. There are a variety of styles to choose from, and you can purchase kits that contain hardware and materials to install these covers yourself. In this project, we'll guide you through steps to hanging a retractable awning: a versatile, convertible top you can pop up for sun exposure, or flip down to go under cover.

The Dirt

Most kits come with a mounting board you affix to the house so the awning is not attached directly to siding. If your kit does not contain a mounting board, purchase a ledger board for this purpose. Because you are adding a fixture to the side of your home, you must secure it properly. Siding alone is not strong enough to support the weight of an awning when it is fully extended. A swift wind could destroy the cover and take chunks of your home's surface with it. Use a stud finder and always affix mounting boards or other hardware (screws, nails, and so forth) to structural points: joists, studs, or headers.

While you're finding the sweet spot to insert your mounting board, remember you don't want to hammer or drill into wiring or plumbing lines. Lines should be centered in wall studs, so you can penetrate the stud up to one inch. You will have to figure how thick the siding and sheathing are to be able to figure your fastener length.

AN AWNING CREATES a cozy dining space and provides shelter from the elements.

Preliminaries

As with any kit, read directions carefully before assembling the awning, and double-check that all parts are included. Careful measurements will ensure that your awning provides the coverage you desire without blocking views or cramping headroom.

Your instructions will indicate the awning's pitch height, which is how far the awning drops down when it is fully extended. When determining where to attach your mounting board and brackets, first decide where you want the brim of the awning to fall. Allow for plenty of headroom. You'll want to enter and exit the covered space without ducking under the awning brim. And you don't want guests to feel claustrophobic under the cover. Consider these variables when deciding where you want the awning brim to fall. Then, add the pitch height to this measurement for the total height. (For example, 6 feet headroom [1.8 m] plus 1 foot [0.3 m] pitch height for a total of 7 feet [2.1 m].) This final measurement is where you attach the awning to your house.

Supplies

- **Stud finder**
- **Power drill**
- **Phillips screwdriver**
- **Wrench**
- **Level**
- **Tape measure**
- **Chalk**
- **Mounting board (in kit), or lumber**

Steps

1. According to kit instructions, determine where you will hang the mounting board and awning brackets by figuring in pitch height. (See Preliminaries.) Using your tape measure and chalk, mark this height on your home's siding with X's.

2. Locate structural points with a stud finder. Mark these with X's.

3. Using a level, draw a straight line where you will attach the mounting board to the home. (You will drill awning brackets into this board, according to instructions.)

4. Before hanging the mounting board, drive in awning brackets. Refer to your kit for spacing measurements.

5. Next, hang the mounting board.

6. Proceed with kit instructions, securing the awning to brackets.

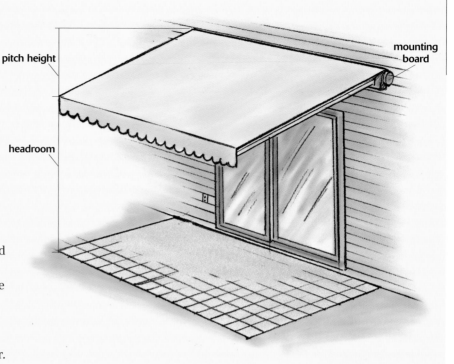

pitch height

mounting board

headroom

MEASURE CAREFULLY.
Allow for headroom, and consider peripheral views when deciding how far you want your awning to hang.

PROJECT PAIRINGS

LOOKING FOR COVERAGE and interest? Try these projects:

Window Boxes   102
Colorful planters attach to your home and spruce up neutral siding.

Perfect Pergola   138
Your patio will feel like a room with this overhead structure.

Dining al Fresco   204
Outdoor dining rooms are intimate, casual, and completely personal.

PROJECT

Build a Shed

When lawn equipment, tools, and planting supplies take over the garage, it's time to consider expanding your storage by annexing some extra real estate for your outdoor toys. A shed provides much-needed space for landscape essentials, and the structure can actually boost your property value if you treat it like an addition to the home. (Think shutters, skylights, and even dedicated spaces inside for storage or hobbies.)

Relax, the project is not as difficult as it seems. You can purchase shed kits that include the lumber, hardware, and specific instructions you'll need to erect a sturdy, attractive shed. This project provides pointers to help you choose the shed that meets your needs.

The Dirt

Search "shed kit" on the Internet, and a laundry list of results will provide you with more options than you thought available. Sure, these offers provide pictures and easy online ordering. But you can't see, touch, or inspect the product before purchasing it. And this is critical. Purchase your shed kit at a hardware, lumber, or home and garden store that carries kits and staffs professionals who can provide advice. Before purchasing a kit, conduct a checkup of the materials and overall panel construction. Observe the thickness of lumber, and be sure it is treated. Is the flooring high quality, and what is the overlap structure of panels? Thick flooring will bear the weight of heavy equipment, and snug panels prevent water leakage. Essentially, you must check for the integrity of the components. Unless you have access to a large truck, the kit will need to be delivered. Decide on where the parts will reside until the shed is constructed.

As you choose a kit, consider the size, how you will use the shed, and what features are important for you.

CONSTRUCT an attractive outbuilding to store supplies, equipment, and other gardening necessities.

YOU CAN MAXIMIZE storage by hanging shelves and hooks on the inside and outside walls.

What's the Function?

How will you use the shed? If gardening is your primary outdoor pursuit, a shed provides a convenient shelter for storing pots and can be equipped with a workspace for planting and related activities. You'll want skylights or windows so the shed gets light exposure and fresh air. Or, perhaps your main priority is to

remove the stuff from your garage (i.e., lawn mower, trimmer, tools). In this case, you may prefer that the shed not have windows, so it is secure and its contents aren't visible. And certainly, you can use a shed for storage and hobbies. Plan on building a larger structure and dedicating areas to specific equipment.

As you consider functionality, you may realize a need for electrical outlets or lighting fixtures in your shed. You can bury electrical cables underground or run them overhead. Regardless, consult with an electrician to help you manage this job. You'll want him or her to evaluate the site and assist with electrical installations.

Size Up Your Stuff

Shed kits look giant in the store, especially considering their proportion compared to bolts and screws in nearby aisles. But looks are deceiving, and you don't want to purchase and build a kit that is too small. You'll end up jamming equipment and tools into the shed and unloading half of its contents every time you need to reach something wedged in the back. Your shed should allow enough room so you can walk in, find what you need, and easily access it.

Evaluate how much space you need by laying out everything you plan to store in the new shed. Space out machines so you can walk between them. Stake the area and attach string to stakes to form a square. (This resembles the outline of your future shed.) Measure the

ADD EXTRA STORAGE shelves or a loft in this tall shed (left). A lean-to style is handy for tucking away everyday items (right).

Before you build, call the city building department or check city ordinances to determine whether you must file a permit. Also be aware of homeowners' association policies that may prohibit sheds and outbuildings.

THIS SOLAR GREEN-HOUSE-STYLE SHED doubles as a storage unit (top, left). A large door on this portable shed allows for easy access to lawn equipment (top, right). A peaked roof accommodates tall equipment. The appealing style makes this shed a second home for tools (bottom).

space. Your dimensions may measure up to 14 by 16 feet (4.3 by 4.9 m) if you plan to store a riding mower and an arsenal of equipment. Better to know this before you decide on the compact 10- by 10-foot (3- by 3-m) model.

Preliminaries

Choose a site that is convenient, and if possible, on level ground. You can always excavate the area. Follow the steps in Brick Paver Patio on page 154 for preparing a foundation. You can build your shed on a concrete slab, but you must allow for frost heave. Many times, a raised deck-style floor is ideal.

A note on instructions: read and reread them. Each step is a manageable task if you understand how the parts fit together as a whole. Before you break out the hammer, take time and care to review all kit contents and arrange them neatly in your work area so you create an organized assembly line. Now, you're ready for production!

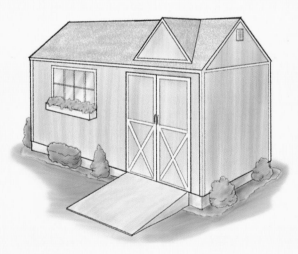

PROJECT PAIRINGS

THE FOLLOWING PROJECTS can help you make the most of your shed:

PROJECT

Organize Your Shed

The garden shed is a popular drop spot for equipment, toys, tools, or any sort of yard miscellany that needs shelter or a hiding place out of plain view. In fact, garden shed is a misnomer for many of us. Over time, the outbuilding becomes a catchall, cluttered like a stuffed closet begging for a garage sale. But how convenient is a shed if you can't find the supplies you store inside?

Time for a cleanout and re-org. (Yes, this probably will require downsizing some of your shed's inventory.) An organized shed that makes best use of space will hold more, but most importantly, you'll be able to access your belongings without dumping half of the shed's contents onto your lawn in the process. Consider this project your shed makeover checklist.

The Dirt

Before you organize, you must clean out. Empty your shed and categorize its contents: tools, gardening, hobbies, sports equipment, power equipment, automotive supplies, and so forth. Depending on how you use the shed, you may find that the space serves diverse purposes. The idea is to compartmentalize items into designated areas of your shed.

After dividing items into piles, evaluate the contents. Recycle broken items or products that are expired. (Be sure to dispose of chemicals and oils properly.) Take stock of tools. Gradually, mountains will deflate into manageable piles. Perhaps it's a good time to plan that yard sale you've been considering, after all.

Next, decide how you will use the shed. Do you want it to hold automotive tools and toys, or will you dedicate this space to only gardening or just lawn equipment? Only return items to the shed that fall into the desired focus. Do bicycles belong in the shed, or is there space in the garage? Come up with a plan B for piles that you won't replace in the shed.

Now, you're ready to organize.

FIND WHAT YOU NEED in a shed equipped with functional storage solutions.

Store gasoline in airtight, approved containers and keep away from moisture and off the ground.

Preliminaries

If you're on an organizing rampage, it's tempting to cruise the aisles of a home store and splurge on handy containers, hooks, and shelves. You'll find plenty of boxes, trays, and all-out storage systems to manage the clutter in your shed, and you can spend as much on the organization products as you did the raw materials to build the shed. But wait. Don't buy until you clean out the shed and determine the size, number, and type of items you need to store. Choose storage that fits your stuff.

Supplies

- **Hooks**
- **Hose organizer**
- **Slatwall**
- **Peg board**
- **Clear plastic bins in various sizes**
- **Shelving units**
- **Work surface**

Steps

1. Clean out your shed. Divide items into piles, and sort out belongings you no longer need or use. Choose a focus for the shed, and find other storage areas for items that don't fit into this category.

2. Decide where you will place each category of supplies in your shed. Keep gardening supplies in one corner, tools on a certain wall, equipment in another area, and miscellaneous items on dedicated shelves. Essentially, you are creating rooms within your shed where you can easily find your belongings.

3. Fill walls. Anything that isn't on four wheels and doesn't stand on its own can be hung from hooks attached to Peg-Board or slatwalls, or stored on shelves and in drawers. Clear plastic bins allow you to view contents, and these can be easily put away on shelves. Cabinets cover up clutter and serve as great spaces to keep gardening supplies.

4. Leave plenty of room to walk around equipment stored on the ground, namely your lawnmower. Store them off to the side or in the back of the shed where they won't act as barriers. If your shed is a step up from the ground, consider installing a ramp so you can easily roll equipment in and out of the shed.

PROJECT PAIRINGS

TRY THESE complementary projects:

Window Boxes   102

Disguise your shed as a guest house by creating window boxes to spruce up its appearance.

Your Shed, a Retreat   170

Beyond organizing your shed, you can convert it into a comfortable outbuilding where you can work or relax.

Doghouse   172

Outbuildings are ideal homes for pets. Make this colorful one for your back yard.

Your Shed, a Retreat

A WELL-APPOINTED SHED may be mistaken for a guesthouse. This outbuilding serves as a remote living room hideaway.

Shed...what shed? Forget half-empty paint cans and rusty tool boxes—erase images of greasy lawn equipment and peg boards cluttered with odds and ends. In search of a private getaway, interesting home office, or outdoor, above-ground version of the quintessential "man basement," luxury sheds wired with technology accommodate homeowners who use them for everything but backyard equipment.

Consider the possibilities a basic outbuilding presents: an airy space to enjoy morning coffee and nature; an inspiring workspace and creative alternative to the corporate cubicle; a media-equipped hideaway; a swank lounge or entertainment space. You can convert your shed into a retreat by souping it up with all the comforts of home. Consider the suggestions in this project, and dream up your own ways to personalize the good, old shed.

The Dirt

Renovating a shed is really no different than building an addition to your home. You may want electrical wiring, access to cable and or Internet services, finishes on walls and floors, and accessories to dress up the place, not to mention comfortable furniture. What makes a shed special is its seclusion from other rooms in the home. To access it, you walk outdoors and enter a new environment. This sense of getting away, departing the norm, and escaping to a private venue is the lure of today's luxury shed.

Preliminaries

How will you reach your shed? Connect this freestanding structure to your garden, a patio, or your back porch. By creating a path, you establish a transition from your home to the shed-room. This hints that the outbuilding is not an afterthought for equipment storage, but an intentional room as functional and important as a study or den.

Steps

1. Surface details. Yes, you can drywall the interior of your shed. In fact, you'll want to insulate it if you plan to use the space year-round in cooler climates. If you opt for warm weather use, paint the studs and sheathing for a cottagelike feel. For an earthy appeal, leave the walls alone. Instead, hang photographs or art to suit your taste. Also consider floors. You can stain a wood-plank surface and toss in a rug to add color, or choose among the wide selection of tile products on the market.

2. Warm the interior. The same features that add depth and comfort to a room in your home also personalize a shed. Hang window treatments, whether basic vertical blinds or vintage lace appointments. A simple swath of material on a bamboo curtain rod is rustic, but more refined than an unfinished frame.

3. Get wired. First address electricity issues. A luxury shed calls for light fixtures and outlets to plug in computers, televisions, and other appliances. If the shed serves as a workspace, you'll surely want a coffeemaker, and why not add a minifridge to your "chill" room? Call an electrician to help you with these jobs. The other aspect of wiring your shed involves Internet access. A small investment in a wireless router will connect a home-based business (ahem, shed-based business) to the outside world.

4. Furniture and fixings. If your shed is secure, insulated, and protected from moisture, there is no reason you can't place the same furniture you'd purchase for your living room in this detached space. Consider waterproof fabrics that won't fade from sun exposure. Of course, you can always retire indoor furniture to your luxury shed if you aren't worried about wear.

5. Dream on! These suggestions will get you started. Once you spend time in your shed-away-from-home, you'll surely come up with other design features to define the interesting space.

PROJECT PAIRINGS

TREAT YOUR SHED like a guesthouse and add these features:

Container Planting Clinic   104
Cluster potted plants at your shed entrance.

Lay a Path   124
A walkway leads the way to your shed retreat.

Garden Benches   140
Build one for inside, or place the bench in a nearby garden.

PROJECT

Doghouse

This playful, Snoopy-style doghouse is a colorful addition to a backyard space. Painted with whimsical spots (just like Spot) and adorned with miniature shutters and window boxes, the attractive pet "cottage" will tempt your children to name it their clubhouse. Here, we'll show you how to make this sweet summer home for your pet.

The Dirt

While a brightly painted doghouse is a cute accessory to a backyard landscape design, it does need to be practical for Fido. The type of doghouse constructed here is great for shelter from the sun and rain for a medium large dog. It isn't meant as year-round living quarters for an outdoor dog. A four-season doghouse is just large enough to fit the dog, since its main warming system is your pet's body heat. To prepare a doghouse for winter, include a baffle door and insulation.

But this project is still a great hangout for the puppy in nice weather. You can customize the house to the dog—got a dachshund? Make a long and skinny house. A great Dane? Double the size of this house. You may wish to decorate the doghouse with shutters, spots that mimic your dog's coat, or even fencing and a mailbox so it has its own backyard. Want to try your hand at siding or stucco? Try it on a small scale by making the doghouse match your home. Just be careful to place the doghouse in a safe area, away from the driveway or high-traffic areas.

Preliminaries

This project includes plenty of options, so choose the features that make sense for your pet. Shingles are not required. You can paint the house, or leave it to weather. The grooved exterior plywood comes in a variety of groove widths. We used the 4-inch (10.2-cm) width because it looks best on the small house. If you are going to side the house with another material, use exterior grade plywood instead of the more expensive grooved plywood.

The parts have been laid out to keep the grooves running up and down on the finished house, and to have the grooves centered on the front and back peaks. Take care with measuring, cutting, and making square corners to have a nicely finished product. Refer to **Figure 1** (page 174) for an overview of the house construction.

Supplies
- **Circular saw**
- **Drill**
- **Jigsaw**
- **Carpenter's square**
- **Paintbrush and paint**
- **Sandpaper**
- **Nontoxic preservative (linseed oil)**
- **Shingles (optional)**
- **4 x 8 foot $^{19}\!/_{32}$" (121.9 x 243.8 x 1.5 cm) grooved exterior siding (2)**
- **4 x 4 foot $^{15}\!/_{32}$" (121.9 x 121.9 x 1.2 cm) sanded exterior plywood (1)**
- **8-foot 2 x 4 (243.8 x 3.8 x 8.9 cm) (2)**
- **6-foot 2 x 2 (182.9 x 3.8 x 3.8 cm) (2)**
- **8-foot pressure treated 2 x 4 (243.8 x 3.8 x 8.9 cm) (2)**
- **8-foot cedar 1 x 4 (243.8 x 1.9 x 8.9 cm) (1)**
- **Nonstaining deck screws**
- **Goggles and hearing protection**

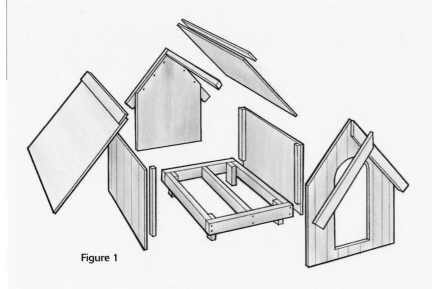

Figure 1

Steps

1. Consult the cutting diagram for laying out cuts on the siding.

2. From the pressure treated 2 x 4 (3.8 x 8.9 cm), cut the two base sides and one center joist at 33" (83.8 cm). Cut the front and back pieces at 30" (76.2 cm). Cut the legs at 6" (15.2 cm).

3. Lap the front and back base boards over the sides and attach with 2½" (64 mm) deck screws. Center the center joist between the front and back baseboards and attach with screws. Attach the legs in the four corners so they are flush with the top edge of the base.

4. Cut the floor panel from the plywood at 30 x 36" (76.2 x 91.4 cm). Align the floor panel on top of the base. Attach the floor to the base with 1¼" (32 mm) deck screws.

5. Cut the house pieces from the grooved plywood. The sides are 22½" tall x 36" wide (57.2 x 91.4 cm).The front and back are 38" (96.5 cm) tall at the peak and 31¼" (79.4 cm) wide. The diagonal cut for the peak begins at 22½" (57.2 cm) On one peaked piece, mark the doorway aligned with the middle groove. Mark a line 3½" (8.9 cm) up from the bottom. This is the bottom of the door. Mark the doorway sides 14" (35.6 cm) apart, centered over the middle groove. Use a compass or a round object to draw the arched door top. Drill a starter hole in the field of the door and cut out the door with a jigsaw.

6. Cut the four corner studs from the 2 x 2 at 18½" (3.8 x 3.8 x 47 cm). Align a stud at the front and back edges of both sides. Align the top of the stud with the top of the side. Attach the sides to the studs with 1¼" (32 mm) deck screws.

7. Attach the sides to the base. The bottom of the side will overlap the base. Drive 1¼" (32 mm) deck screws through the bottom of the side into the base **(Figure 2)**.

8. Attach the front and the back, driving 1¼" (32 mm) deck screws through and bottoms edges into the base, and through the sides into the studs.

9. Cut the ridge board from the 2 x 2 at 36" (3.8 x 3.8 x 91.4 cm). Attach the ridge board between the front and the back, aligned with the peaks, using 1¼" (32 mm) deck screws.

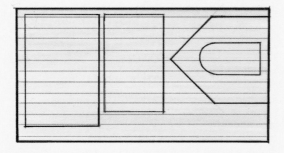

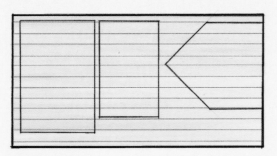

Cutting Diagram

Carefully measure and pencil-in parts on the plywood before cutting. Refer to the cutting diagram, which is laid out to make best use of the grooved exterior siding. Use a circular saw and a long saw guide to make quality cuts.

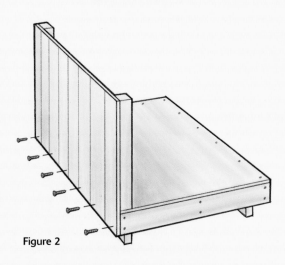

Figure 2

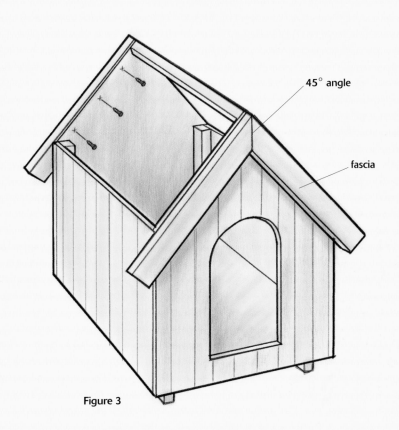

45° angle

fascia

Figure 3

10. Cut the fascia from the 2 x 4 at 28" (3.8 x 8.9 x 71.1 cm), mitering one end at 45°. Attach the fascia to the front and back peaks, driving 1¼" (32 mm) deck screws from inside the house (**Figure 3**).

11. Cut the roof panels to size from the grooved siding. One panel is 28⅞" x 42" (73.3 x 106.7 cm) and the other is 29½" x 42" (74.9 x 106.7 cm). Center the smaller panel over the house, aligning the top edge with the peak. Attach to the fascia and ridge board with 1¼" (32 mm) deck screws. The larger panel overlaps the smaller panel. Align it and attach.

12. Cut the roof ridge boards from the 1 x 4 cedar at 42" (1.9 x 8.9 x 106.7). Using the circular saw and an edge guide, rip ¾" (1.9 cm) from the edge of one roof ridge. Attach the roof ridge boards to the roof peak, overlapping them in the opposite direction from the roof board overlaps.

13. Finish the dog house as desired.

PROJECT PAIRINGS

NOW THAT YOUR PET has a comfortable home, add these fun backyard features to the mix:

Attract Butterflies   **90**
If you don't have a four-footed friend, you can still create an animal habitat.

Build a Shed   **164**
Consider it a larger version of the doghouse, and designed for your hobbies and tools.

Just for Kids!   **210**
Create a children's play area with a simple A-frame design and basic construction.

PART FIVE

Setting Mood

The outdoor living room is an attractive concept for those of us who want an escape without the hassle. No travel time necessary, no reservations required. All you need is a slice of time and a comfortable environment, where nature serves as the backdrop and the features you incorporate set the mood. Whether your property is entertainment central or a quiet retreat, these projects will transform your backyard into an appealing destination.

PROJECT

Create a Pond

Water enchants. Its lapping sound kneads away tension, and its looking-glass surface invites us to stop, reflect, and relax. In a landscape, water serves as a focal point, a backyard oasis. Ponds are a serene centerpiece that transform a basic backyard into something striking and special. Aqua-loving plants add interest to garden-variety landscapes, and the ecological benefits that ponds lend to your space make this project an aesthetic and sustainable venture.

Even better news: There is not a lot of work involved in installing such a high-impact feature. Materials available today ease the process, and you can feasibly build an attractive pond in a weekend. Depending on the size, shape, and location of the pond, you have a few different options for pond liners. There are materials that cater to every price point, so don't let a pond's exotic look fool you into thinking the project carries a hefty price tag. Garden stores, retail outlets, and companies that specialize in pond products stock an array of pond liners, pumps, and materials to make the job easy. You can also purchase kits—a convenient option that we'll explore in this project.

The Dirt

You know the saying: location, location, location. Yes, location *is* a big deal when planning a pond. Not just any clear space is suitable for a water feature. To position your pond to stay clean and healthy, you must consider all the obstacles in your backyard.

- **Where are trees** located? Do roots protrude?
- **What areas** are exposed to direct sunlight, and for how long?
- **Is your property** on a slope? Is there a level area in your yard that is appropriate for a pond?
- **Where do you** like to relax outdoors? Do you want to view the pond from a patio, or would you like to create a separate "room" in your backyard with seating and plant life around the pond?

Protruding tree roots can make digging difficult and you risk damaging the tree if you disturb its root system too much. Also, by placing a pond directly under a tree, it will collect leaves and other debris, which means you'll be cleaning your pond often.

Examine your back yard for shade and sun, and note spaces where there is a combination of both. This is important because most aquatic plants need four to six hours of direct sunlight, and mature tree canopies can block rays for most of the day in some cases.

Also notice the grade. You obviously do not want to install a pond on a slope, unless you plan to build up the grade, and that process creates more work and can require assistance from a professional.

Finally, decide where you like to spend your time outdoors. You want to enjoy the pond, so place it in a location where it is visible from a patio or seating area. Think about ways to position the feature so you can take advantage of its aesthetic appeal year-round. Do you want to see the pond from indoors? Water features add interest to a living room, as well, if you can see the pond from a window.

Aquatic Plants

Building a water feature into your landscape expands your planting options to include aqua-loving varieties, such as water lilies, irises, ornamental grasses, and water hyacinths. With water-garden plants, you can create a diverse ecosystem in your backyard and maintain a clean, healthy pond.

There are various types of plants you can grow in or near water. Some stay submerged, others float, and you'll find various species that thrive in shallow water near the edge of the pond. Incorporate a mix of plants to preserve your pond's ecological balance: oxygenating plants (underwater plants that absorb nutrients and carbon dioxide); surface fixtures like water lilies, which shade the area; and bog plants that consume nitrogen and phosphates and also help keep ponds clean. Most aquatic plants grow in pots that you place at the bottom of your pond.

If you plan to grow aquatic plants, to make sure your pond is deep enough to accommodate them. You can purchase plants for shallow, medium, and deep water. Deep-water plants will require at least 6 feet (1.8 meters) of water to thrive, whereas shallow-water plants are hardy in an average 1-foot (0.3-meter) water depth. Do your homework before digging the pond so you don't limit your options.

Pond Maintenance

All ponds require maintenance to sustain their delicate ecological balance. By keeping up with basic tasks like trimming plants and removing leaves, you can prevent algae buildup and other problems down the road. Here are some pond clean up tips to observe during seasons when the pond is in use.

- **Remove** leaves and debris from pond surface.
- **Weed out** invasive plants and trim unruly ones; aim for 40 to 60 percent plant coverage.
- **Replenish** pond water during drought conditions, when levels will run low.
- **Clean** algae from pumps and filters; do not clean out biological filters, which will destroy algae-fighting bacteria that live there.
- **Control** runoff: avoid fertilizing areas that may drain into the pond, as fertilizer will throw of the balance of your pond and promote algae growth.

Pond Filters and Pumps

You can build a small pond without a pump or filter, but you will likely invite water quality problems. To maintain oxygen levels in a pond, consider installing a small waterfall or spray jet—anything to keep the water moving. Or, play it safe an put in a filtration system.

There are two types of filtration systems: mechanical and biological. Some are two-in-one systems. Mechanical systems filter debris and algae, while biological filters oxygenate the pond so beneficial bacteria will thrive. Biological filters are essential if your pond contains fish, because these systems break down pollutants and toxic ammonia from fish waste. Be careful not to clean biological filters or you will destroy resident algae-fighting bacteria.

For small ponds without fish, mechanical filters are sufficient. You can purchase a submersible (internal) filter and set it into a pond, away from mud and plant material that can clog it. Be sure the discharge hose stays submerged. You also can hook this hose to a fountain, waterfall, or other spraying feature.

You need a pump to operate a filter. Make sure the pump will handle filter requirements. Your best bet is to talk to a pond professional. Check package labels, and err on the side of more pump power.

Preliminaries

Select a site for your pond based on your property diagram, considering shade/sun and obstacles. Use a garden hose or rope to outline the pond shape; you can adjust it into smooth, natural curves. Take your time and play with various shapes and arrangements, referring to your diagram if necessary. Step back from the shape you create and be sure it complements the surroundings.

This project outlines how to create a small ovoid pond with a shelf for plantings. It uses a flexible rubber liner with small flagstones on its lip. Have a plan for using the dirt excavated from your pond area. You may want to fill in low areas in your yard, create raised beds, or make a berm. The pond has a border, which masks the pond liner and finishes the pond edge

Size the rubber pond liner to fit the excavated area. To determine the size, draw an imaginary square around the pond perimeter. Measure the length and width of the square. Then, multiply the pond's maximum depth by two, and add 3 feet (1 meter) for the shelf and extra room for the liner to settle. The sum of these measurements is the size you should cut your liner.

Supplies
- **Pond liner**
- **Garden hose**
- **Spade**
- **Shovel**
- **Sand**
- **Wheelbarrow**
- **A straight piece of lumber**
- **Carpenter's level**
- **Flagstone or decorative edging**

Steps

1. Mark the outline of your pond with a hose or rope. Using a spade, cut around the outline of the pond. Remove dirt, excavating the pond area to a depth of about 10" to 12" (25.4 to 30.5 cm). This is the depth of the pond shelf.

2. Measure in 10" to 12" (25.4 to 30.5 cm) from the pond sides. This marks the center of the pond. Excavate the center of the pond another 1' to 2' (30 to 60 cm). Remove all debris and rocks from the pond floor to prevent puncturing the liner.

3. Once you dig out the pond area, place a level on top of a straight piece of lumber across the pond. Check for level all around the pond rim. Remove or add dirt until the pond is even across the top **(Figure 1)**.

4. Dig a shallow bed around the perimeter of the pond, just wide enough to accommodate the flagstone or your chosen border.

5. Spread a 2" (5.1 cm) layer of sand on the pond bottom and shelf so the liner will lay on a smooth surface. Then, carefully place the liner into the pond bed by positioning it over the hole and slowly lowering it into place until it drops to the bottom. Use helpers for this step; the liner is much easier to handle with a couple of extra hands.

6. Place some stones around the perimeter of the pond to hold down the liner.

7. Gradually fill the pond, while smoothing out any wrinkles in the liner as the water level rises. After the pond is full, remove the stones and allow time for the liner to settle.

8. Trim the liner so it forms a 4" to 6" (10.2 to 15.2 cm) border around the perimeter of the pond. Finish the pond by laying flagstones around the perimeter. You can build up the stone using several layers for a raised look or use a single layer so the pond is even with the surface **(Figure 2)**.

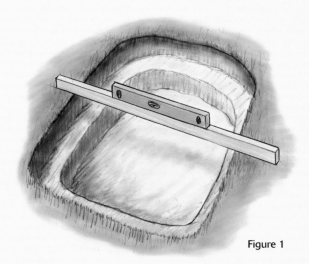

Figure 1

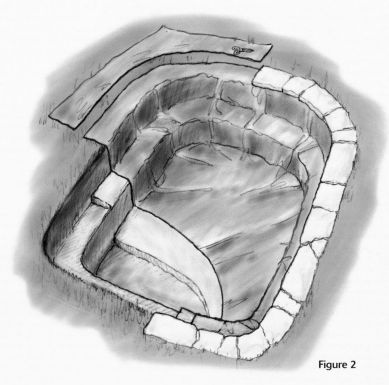

Figure 2

PROJECT PAIRINGS

ENJOY YOUR POND environment by adding these features:

Garden Benches   140
Sit, relax, take in the atmosphere of your outdoor living room.

Fountain Water Feature   182
A gurgling miniature version of your pond is portable for patios.

PROJECT

Fountain Water Feature

Gurgling water fountains appeal to the senses. Their playful splashing sounds and peaceful, constant murmur add atmosphere to intimate spaces such as patios and gardens. Plug one in and relax by your portable pond.

Fountains range from ornate marble to sleek Zen styles. Because water features are quite popular, you'll find a selection at retailers, but you'll empty your wallet for some of these ready-made fixtures. You can make your own fountain out of a terra-cotta pot for a fraction of the cost. All you need is a focal point location close to a power source, a terra-cotta container, and a submersible pump. You'll find that these portable water features are ideal for small spaces, and they complement nearly every garden.

The Dirt

The pump is the voice of your fountain, if you will. You can choose pumps that gently bubble, spit, or spray water—some spew with dramatic water works, while others are subtle tricklers, perfect for meditative environments. Just be sure the pump you choose is submersible with a flow rate of about 60 gallons (227.4 L) per hour. This is enough power for the medium-sized fountain pot you'll create.

Choose a container that is about 20 inches (50.8 cm) tall and 30 inches (76.2 cm) wide for this project. This is large enough to serve as a centerpiece of a deck or garden area. Arrange your fountain near a container garden so it becomes one of the bunch. These versatile water features lend themselves to imaginative design.

Preliminaries

Choose a location for your fountain that is near a power source. That way, you can plug in your submersible pump. If you want to position the water feature in a garden space, purchase a weather-ready extension cord designed for outdoor use and bury the cable along a bed line. Just be sure your connections don't spoil the aesthetic quality of this project.

YOU CAN USE A VARIETY of containers for fountains. We'll show you how to turn a terra-cotta pot into a water feature, but explore other options such as this decorative pot.

■ Watch fountain water levels during hot, dry weather. Water can evaporate quickly in the summer, especially in shallow fountains. Refill the fountain weekly, and consider purchasing a pump that shuts off automatically when water levels are too low, so you don't risk burning out the pump motor.

■ Add a couple of tablespoons of bleach to your fountain each week to prevent algae growth. If your fountain is an attraction for wildlife, choose an algaecide that is safe for animals.

Supplies

- **Terra-cotta pot**
- **Drill**
- **⅝" (16 mm) drill bit**
- **Round rasp**
- **Ruler**
- **Submersible pump**
- **Aerosol acrylic sealer**
- **Silicone sealant**

Steps

1. Select a site and choose a container.

2. If the container has a drainage hole, determine if it is large enough for the pump cord plug to fit through. If not, enlarge the hole with the rasp. If the pot has no hole, soak the pot in water for an hour, then drill a hole in the side or bottom of the pot. Use the rasp to enlarge the hole until the plug fits through.

3. If the pot is unglazed, seal the inside with two coats of acrylic sealant. (If you have soaked it to drill a hole, allow it to dry thoroughly before sealing.)

4. Place the pump in a bucket filled with water and test that it works.

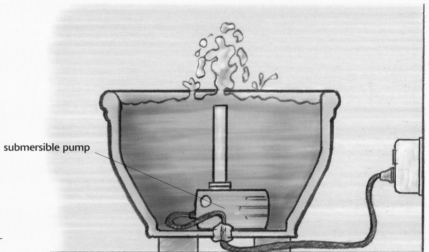

submersible pump

5. Place the pump inside the pot and feed the cord through the hole. You may need to place the pump atop bricks so that it is centered and the cord can still go through the hole. Seal the hole around the cord marine-grade silicone sealant.

6. Fill the pot with water, leaving room at the top for water to splash without pouring over the side.

PROJECT PAIRINGS

THESE PROJECTS will also enhance the mood of your landscape:

Maximizing a Small Space　　　　　　**28**
Learn other design clues to enhance a modest-sized yard.

Backyard Fire Pit　　　　　　**198**
You have the water, now add another earthen element: fire.

PROJECT

Install Landscape Lighting

Capture nature's nightlife with low-voltage landscape lighting, and turn on your property's after-five appeal. Landscape lighting extends the usability of outdoor spaces, and its benefits are threefold: aesthetics, value, and safety. Low-voltage lighting can accent your home's architectural character and highlight favorite landscape features. It pumps up curb appeal, and lighting dark areas will discourage unwanted visitors from invading your privacy.

Most of all, lighting creates drama. The contrast between light and shadow introduces new shapes and angles at night—a different perspective from daytime views. Also, lighting truly allows you to capitalize on your landscape investment because you can enjoy outdoor features year-round, from the view of a window, or while relaxing on your deck.

Installing low-voltage landscape lighting is safe and simple, thanks to today's packaged kits and widely available architectural-grade fixtures. We'll show you how.

The Dirt

Low-voltage fixtures can subtly illuminate outdoor features. But done in excess, lighting is a bold mistake. Less is more. Gradually add lights then step back and see whether your fixture arrangement illuminates dark spots. Don't place lights too closely together, allow the beam to fill in space between each fixture. You don't want to light up your property like a ballpark, and your neighbors probably wouldn't appreciate that either.

Natural night-lighting is achieved by layering lights, and installing the right fixtures in the right places. Choose spotlights for intense, specific uplighting and path lights to illuminate walkways and feature plants. Think in tiers: spotlight focal points, softly illuminate paths, and shine surface lights on porches or landings.

Fixtures

Be sure that the fixtures you purchase are rated as water-resistant and are approved by the Underwriter's Laboratory (UL) for outdoor use. Never use interior lights outdoors. Also, if you plan to add lights to a water feature, ensure that fixtures are labeled for this application.

You can purchase lighting sets or separate fixtures from retail home outlets and select garden stores. Kits generally include fixtures, a wire, a controller (to turn lights off and on), and a transformer. Fixtures sold a la carte are convenient for adding onto an existing lighting project or if you want to illuminate a single feature. Also available are higher-end architectural grade fixtures, which come in a variety of contemporary finishes, such as brushed copper. These luminaries are built to last, and you can expect them to light your landscape for 10 to 15 years. Kits generally fizzle after a few years. With lighting, you get what you pay for.

Mainly, your fixture choices will depend on your experience and comfort level with low-voltage lighting, and also your expectations for the results. Architectural-grade fixtures generally contain halogen bulbs that cast a white, more focused beam for a natural look. On the other hand, lighting sets provide a quick-and-simple solution for homeowners who want to install path lighting. Both are easy to install as long as you avoid common low-voltage traps (explained below). When purchasing any fixture at a retail store, discuss your plans with an in-house specialist to determine which product is the best fit for your project.

The following fixtures serve specific lighting purposes.

Path lights: Available in a variety of styles and finishes: Tall bollard lights add height; shorter yard lights highlight low plants; and decorative lights in bronze, black and die-cast metal finishes can complement a landscape. Lighting professionals suggest mushroom-capped lights as opposed to pagoda-style path lights often sold in kits. Capped lights direct light downward so you will avoid the airport runway effect. Fixtures should not exceed 2 feet (0.6 meters) in height.

Spotlights: Designed to accent specific features, such as trees and sculpture. The beam is direct and the fixture can be adjusted to accommodate the height of the desired feature. Use discretion with spotlights. Choose a couple of priority features to highlight, and apply shields to lights to avoid glare if they are visible.

Solar lights: A low-maintenance way to light a path, but don't expect the high-impact results you get from low-voltage lighting. The actual fixture looks no different than its cousin, the path light, but the beam from solar lights is not as intense. Because their brightness depends on how much sunlight solar panels soak in during the day, you can't expect consistent light from these fixtures. However, their soft glow is appealing to homeowners who want a quick fix to light a path or low-growing plants.

Specialty lights: A variety of decorative lighting options on the market today provide practical and whimsical ways to add panache to a patio area. For function, mounted lights installed on deck posts illuminate eating and grilling areas. For fun, string nylon lantern lights around a patio or in low-hanging tree branches to create a party atmosphere. Water lights add sparkle to ponds and fountains.

Powering Up

There are a few things about electricity that you need to know to successfully install your low-voltage system. It is important to understand that the length of your low-voltage power line, the wire gauge used, and the wattage maximum of your transformer can affect the performance of your fixtures.

Most kits are fool proof—they give you only the number of fixtures and length of wire the transformer can handle. If you buy fixtures, wire, and transformers separately, know that you need to do some figuring. For example, if you have a 100 watt transformer and you have six 16.5 watt path light fixtures, you can use a maximum of 40 feet of 14 gauge wire without affecting the performance of the fixtures. If

you increase the gauge of the wire to 12 or decrease the number of fixtures, you can double the length of the wire.

The maximum output wattage varies with the transformer model. If you exceed the transformer's maximum wattage, the lighting system will fail. The transformer will convert electricity to the 12-volt level outdoor light-

---

DESIGN TIP

A shielded directional light is a multipurpose fixture. It looks like a juice can with a stake in it, and the light is in the bottom of the can so there is less glare. Mount it under the eaves of buildings, inside gazebos, at the base of sculptures, and near water features.

ing requires. It's generally a good idea to buy a transformer with more capacity than you need so you have the option to add fixtures later. Also, always check the wattage of light fixtures, and add up the total per line to avoid overloading your transformer. For example, a 100-watt transformer will accommodate up to nine 11-watt fixtures or six 16.5-watt fixtures. This is especially important if you are buying single fixtures or adding fixtures to an existing wire.

Also important is that you observe the minimum distance placement for the first fixture. If you place the first fixture too close to the transformer, the bulb will be overloaded and burn out prematurely.

If you have a very large yard and need to run wires hundreds of feet, purchase a transformer with multiple taps of increased voltage. These taps are designed to feed more power to faraway fixtures.

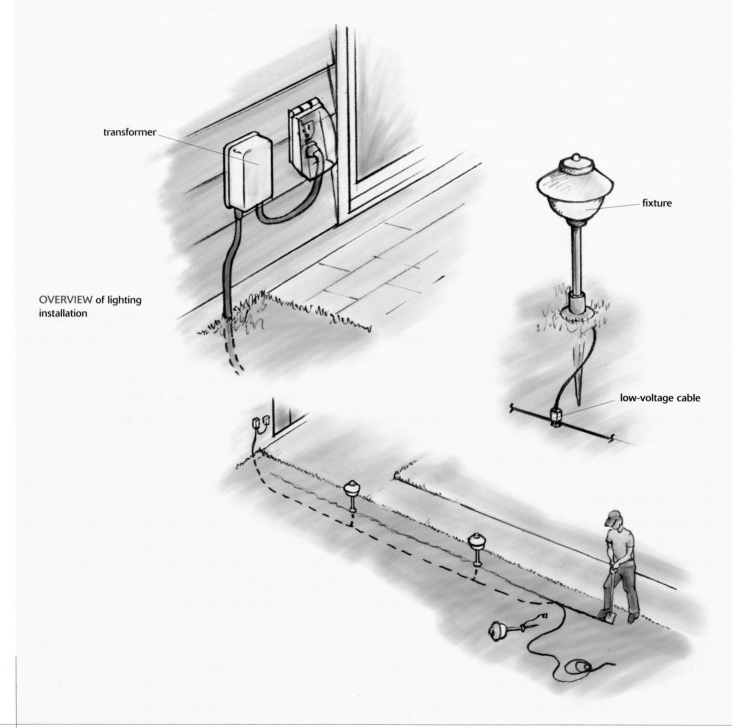

transformer

fixture

OVERVIEW of lighting installation

low-voltage cable

Before digging trenches to hide lighting cables, be sure you know the location of underground wires and pipes. Call your utility company and ask them to mark these spots before you dig.

Preliminaries

Before you begin, use your site map (pages 18 to 21) to plan your lighting installation. Ideally, you will plan lighting as you install other landscape features; but for most homeowners, lighting is an afterthought. This is fine, because low-voltage wires do not need to be buried deeply and simple fixtures can easily be installed in one afternoon. Regardless, this visual aid is an important preinstallation step that will help you lay out a plan for where to place fixtures. This way, you can determine how much wire and how many fixtures to purchase.

- **Choose** a few main focal points you want to highlight at night. These might include a couple of interesting trees, a plant bed, a water feature or walkway you wish to illuminate for guests.
- **Note** available outdoor electrical outlets.
- **Mark** dark spots in corners or behind bushes, and potentially hazardous steps and curbs
- **Plot** where you will place outdoor lights. Eleven-watt bulbs cast 4 feet (1.2 meters) of light, and path lights are generally available in 20 watts or less.

Supplies

- **Outdoor low-voltage cable**
- **Lighting fixtures**
- **Transformer**
- **Timer (optional)**
- **Spade, small shovel, or lawn edger**

Steps

1. Mount the transformer on the house next to an outdoor electrical outlet and at least 12" (30.5 cm) above grade. (Follow directions on package.) Connect the transformer to the outlet.

2. Lay out fixtures and wire. If installing lights near plants that are not yet mature, you'll want to eventually move fixtures out to accommodate growth, so allow some slack.

3. Place fixtures in desired locations. Attach fixtures to the supply wire using the pinch or screw connectors included with the fixtures.

4. Connect the end of the supply wire to the transformer taps, following manufacturer's directions. Turn on the transformer to verify that all fixtures are working properly.

5. Use a spade, small shovel, or lawn edger to create a shallow trench along the bed where you want to bury cable. If you prefer, cut a 45-degree angle in the lawn surface, pry up turf and place cable under the sod blanket.

6. Set the automatic timer (if you choose).

PROJECT PAIRINGS

NOW THAT YOU'VE EXTENDED your time outdoors with lighting, try these projects:

Backyard Fire Pit   198
Light in its many forms induces feelings of peace and relaxation.

Dining al Fresco   204
Lights, candles, texture, color—create an atmosphere for entertaining.

Operation Conceal

What do you see while relaxing on your patio? How about when you look out your kitchen window, or stand in the middle of your back yard? Out of the corner of your eye, do you catch a glimpse of that utility box? Perhaps the view of your neighbor's jumbo kiddie gym set is more action that you wish to experience from the tranquil setting you've tried to create.

Each of us requires a different level of privacy; some of us would immediately call a code red on the last scenario. But all of us have a few eyesores to conceal. Utility meters, trash receptacles, outdoor electrical outlets, even the elements we build ourselves (compost bins) may benefit from a privacy shield. These blots on the landscape mar your view, and the sounds you overhear are equally invasive: traffic, humming air conditioner units, noisy neighbors, or barking dogs.

The good news is there are ways to disguise these distractions. This is Operation Conceal, a mission to help you filter the noise pollution and screen undesirables. Then, we'll show you how to turn prefabricated lattice panels into an inventive curtain for a pergola, front porch, or back deck space.

The Dirt

Many of the projects in this book can be modified and reconstructed to conceal a private space or hide eyesores. You can plant, screen, and mask eyesores. For example, lattice is an excellent material that shields without completely shutting out a view. And, you can install a range of fencing that provides privacy without blocking surroundings completely. Consider the following ideas to help you restore peace and quiet to your backyard retreat.

LATTICE PANELS work as double agents, concealing an undesirable view and providing a backdrop for garden beds.

Plant a Curtain

When choosing plants to serve as a natural fence, height and volume are primary considerations. Depending on the setting, a row of neatly trimmed hedges may form a 4-foot (1.2 m) tall border that serves as a room divider in your outdoor space. Boxwoods are also great low "fences," though they require maintenance. If the idea is to close out a view completely, choose taller 8-foot (2.4-m) evergreens, or cypress that has height.

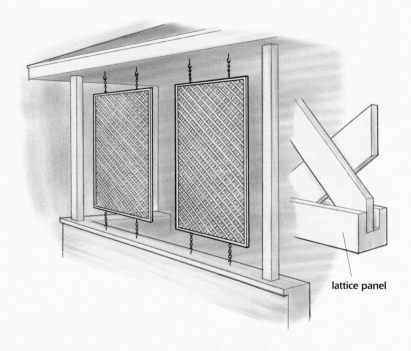

OVERVIEW of porch-mounted lattice panel project

lattice panel

Remember, if you require a year-round privacy screen, choose plant material that will not shed its leaves in winter. Evergreens are ideal for this reason, but they can be slow-growing. Speed may be a priority if you want to fill in the space quickly. You can purchase mature evergreens, which is costly. Or, plant eager growers, such as bamboo. (*See Zen Space on page 118 for tips on training bamboo so it doesn't get too eager.*)

Screen Eyesores

Many times, privacy is gained by creating a screen rather than a solid wall. In such cases, open-weave and lattice-style fences, or a row of tall ornamental grasses, may do the job. Climbing plants supported by a trellis or fence will increase coverage. But beyond creating property borders, you can build covers with lattice to hide all sorts of things. Construct box shapes or containers for concealing necessities, such as trash cans.

On a front porch, outdoor fabric sheers hung on a drapery rod or suspended by sturdy vinyl cord provides an airy touch of privacy. Tie back curtains, or draw them to block intense sun or wind. You can use folding screens for the same purpose. Since they are portable they can be relocated to a deck and used as a background wall to add ambiance to an outdoor dinner party.

Mask Sound

A gurgling water fountain may be just the white noise you need to drown out constant traffic. You can create your own portable feature from terra-cotta pots (see Fountain Water Feature, page 182), or install a pond with a fountain that sprays and splashes. Privacy fences also help soundproof a landscape. Choose masonry, solid stockade and board fences, because they are relatively impermeable and do not contain openings that allow sound to drift through. Plant material buffers will further muffle sound.

Preliminaries

Lattice panels are readily available, attractive, and can be painted and finished to match your home or accent landscape features. This project requires little labor, but provides lots of openings for creative expression. Once you hang a lattice panel from your porch or pergola, you can treat it as you would a wall in your home: hang pictures, weave in fabric, grow flowering clematis. You can even hang small potted plants.

The first order of business is to measure the space, width and height. Purchase already assembled lattice that you can cut to size and finish with lattice edging.

Lattice panel is also available in plastic, which doesn't require painting and won't peel, split, or require repainting.

Supplies

- **Lattice panels**
- **Jigsaw or circular saw**
- **Lattice edging**
- **Try square**
- **Coated 1" (25 mm) panel nails**
- **Drill**
- **Exterior wood glue**
- **Chain**
- **Level**
- **Bolt cutter**
- **S hooks**
- **Eye screws**
- **Paint, stain, or finish of your choice**

Steps

1. Cut the lattice to size using a circular or jig saw. To make straight lines, clamp a long straight edge or straight piece of lumber to the lattice panel to act as a saw guide and to hold to panel rigid.

2. Cut the lattice edging to length, mitering the ends at 45 degrees. To get the proper sizing, mark the grooved side of the edging with the lattice size, then use the try square to measure the 45° angle out (longer) to the flat side.

3. Align one piece of lattice edging on the lattice. Drive panel nails through the edging and through the lattice where it is doubled. If you are using cedar panels and edging, drill $\frac{1}{16}$" (1 mm) pilot holes for the nails to prevent splitting.

4. Apply glue to the mitered corners, and attach the second piece of edging. Continue for the third and fourth pieces of edging. Drill $\frac{1}{16}$" (1 mm) pilot holes from the flat side of the edging across the miter joint. Drive two panel nails per corner to further secure, or locknail, the joint.

5. Drill pilot holes in the top beam of a porch or pergola where you are hanging the screen. Screw the eye screws into the lattice edging. Use the shaft of a screwdriver through the eye to aid in twisting in the screw.

6. Align the lattice screen with the eye screws and mark the placement. Drill pilot holes and screw in eye screws. Hang S hooks from the eye screws. Hang a length of chain from each S hook on the beam, and hang the panel by attaching its S hooks to the chain. Using a bolt cutter, cut the chain to the desired length. Check the screens for level. If they are not level, adjust by screwing in or unscrewing eye screws.

7. Attach a second set of eye screws, S hooks, and chain to the bottom of the screen to prevent it from blowing in the wind.

8. Finish the screen as desired.

PROJECT PAIRINGS

THESE PROJECTS will also help you achieve privacy:

Lath Trellis   130
Build a frame to grow climbing plants that hide views.

Perfect Pergola   138
Hang lattice "curtain" from a pergola to create a private retreat.

Fountain Water Feature   182
Gurgling water disguises outside noises.

Painted Gates

Gates provide a point of entry. They welcome visitors and introduce a garden, landscape, or any private space enclosed by a fence. Gates define an area as special, or mark a territory as off-limits.

Besides their physical purpose and symbolism as a "gateway" to the garden, gates make great landscape embellishments. Painted or weathered, their structure is ideal for growing climbers. (See Vines for Landscapes on page 86.) They also serve as a colorful backsplash to flower beds. In this project, we'll show you how to make a Z-frame gate; but don't feel obligated to pair it with a fence. Gates make a statement of their own.

The Dirt

Gates do require high construction standards, and since they are available in various styles in home improvement stores, you may choose to simply buy the gate and paint it to your liking. The gate in this project is a Z-frame, which is a light, simple construction. A perimeter-frame gate is more solid with its four-cornered frame and diagonal brace, and is appropriate for rugged use.

Support is the key to a sturdy gate. If you plan to attach the gate to a fence, adequate weight distribution is critical. Gateposts must be plumb, and gates must be true, otherwise your awkward gate will catch or drag when opened.

Preliminaries

A gate that will hang from a fence requires careful measurement *before* you purchase hardware (latches and hinges). Record the diameter of your gatepost, and sketch a drawing of your gate. The hardware you choose affects the clearance between your gateposts and the gate frame. Finally, before you attach hardware, consider which way you want the gate to swing.

If your gate is purely aesthetic, serving as a standalone accessory rather than a working entryway to your yard, you can simply construct the Z-gate design without worry of hardware placement. Though you may choose to purchase and attach a latch to the gate for decoration, especially if you find an interesting design.

Supplies

- **Preshaped pickets**
- **2 x 4 lumber (3.8 x 8.9 cm)**
- **1¾" (44 mm) corrosion-resistant deck screws**
- **4-inch (102 mm) deck screws**
- **Tape measure**
- **Level**
- **Carpenter's square**
- **Circular saw**
- **Drill/driver and bits**
- **Bar clamps**
- **Combination square**
- **Paintbrush**
- **Paint, stain, or sealer**
- **Hinge hardware (optional)**
- **Treated cedar or redwood lumber**

WITH OR WITHOUT a fence, garden gates are a pleasing way to say welcome to a landscape.

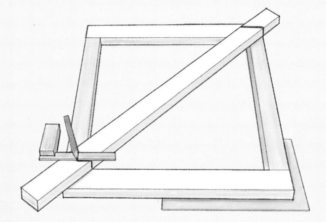

Figure 1

THE DIAGONAL PIECE must reach from the upper corner to the lower corner.

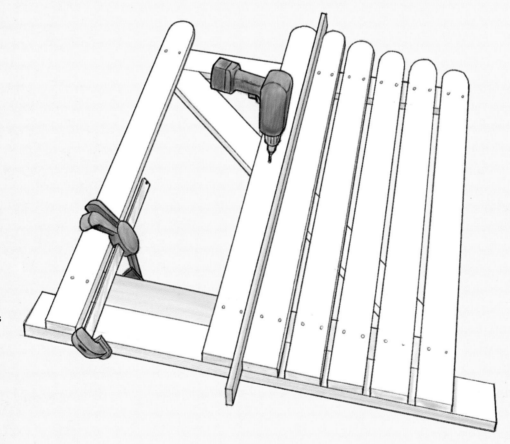

Figure 2

USE A SPACER to help you line up fence boards evenly along the frame.

If gateposts aren't plumb, even them up by attaching a sag rod or wire at the top of the post. Run it diagonally to the lower end of the next post. Tighten the turnbuckle in the middle until the post is aligned.

Steps

1. If you plan to hang the gate on a fence, check both gate posts for plumb using a level. Measure the gate opening, and consult the packaging on hinge and latch hardware. Subtract necessary clearance from the gate opening. This is your gate width. Cut 2 x 4 (3.8 x 8.9 cm) lumber to this length for horizontal braces. (If you plan to prop the gate against a wall, skip step 1 and merely cut braces to desired width of the gate.)

2. Prime, stain, or treat the lumber for the gate frame and pickets. Let dry completely before proceeding.

3. Cut two pieces of 2 x 4 (3.8 x 8.9 cm) lumber scrap to temporarily space horizontal braces. These will align the top and bottom braces of the gate with the bottom and top stringers of the fence.

4. Lay out the frame on a flat work surface with the wide face down. Place the temporary supports between braces. Use a carpenter's square to check the angle of frame corners (90 degrees).

5. Place a 2 x 4 diagonally from one end of the lower brace across to the opposite end of the upper brace. The frame corners and diagonal will make a Z shape. Mark and cut the diagonal brace with a saw **(Figure 1)**.

6. Remove temporary supports. Drill pilot holes through the diagonal brace into the horizontal braces. Drive the 4" (102 mm) deck screws through the diagonal brace into the horizontal braces at a slant (called toe-nailing).

7. Lay out the pickets on your frame, starting flush with one end of the horizontal braces. If making a gate to for an existing fence, match the picket spacing to the existing fence spacing. Arrange the pickets on the gate frame, using the spacer boards to maintain consistency in the gaps. If the last board hangs over your frame, measure the overhang. Divide this measurement by two. Cut this length off the side of each end board. (For example, if the last board overhangs by 1 inch (2.5 cm), cut ½ inch (1.3 cm) off each side of end boards.)

PROJECT PAIRINGS

A GATE COMPLEMENTS these landscape features:

Layering Plant Beds   72
A gate serves as a backdrop to a colorful plant bed.

Cottage Garden Master Plan   76
All gardens of this nature include a gate to symbolize entry.

Operation Conceal   190
Gates can hide eyesores.

Backyard Fire Pit

NOTHING ADDS warmth to an outdoor space like an authentic fire pit.

A crackling fire plays a lively host for outdoor gatherings. There's something meditative about a dancing open flame; it soothes the soul. And when the heat is on, you'll undoubtedly attract s'more lovers to the circle. Inevitably, a fire pit serves as a backyard centerpiece, and the interesting stone you can incorporate into its base creates character in the structure.

You can re-create a campfire setting with this fire pit project, which is best suited for properties with plenty of breathing room for open flames.

The Dirt

Safety plays the primary role in site selection for your fire pit. Choose a space away from trees and shrubs, and at least 25 feet (7.6 m) away from anything combustible. This includes areas where you store power equipment, fuel, and oil for lawn maintenance. Also, because your fire pit will be smoky, you may wish to position it further away from the home. A large backyard with wide open space is an ideal site for a fire pit.

Stone Selection

You can pick and choose stones at a quarry, or order a pallet of stone, which are preselected for quality. You will pay slightly more for the pallet, but you'll also save time. However, a visit to a quarry can be an adventure worth the trip, and the workers there can help you select a variety of face stones and capstones to complete this project. Capstones are flatter, larger smooth stones that will form the top or cap of your fire pit wall. Face stones are smooth or slightly rounded and form the body of the wall, or the face. Be sure to bring the dimensions of your desired fire pit to the quarry, and ask about delivery.

Setting Stone

Setting stones is like working a puzzle. You want stones to fit snugly together, avoiding large joints, or gaps. Also, you should incorporate a variety of stone sizes. Mixing small and large stones accentuates the character of each stone. If you find a stone that isn't quite the size you want, you can always shape it with a chipping hammer. Put on safety glasses, score a light line on the stone with the sharp end of the hammer, then chip the stone with the mallet end. Aim for a running bond pattern by placing one stone over the joint of two stones (see **Figure 2** page 156). When two joints are stacked, the wall is not as strong. This fire is lined with fire brick, which is available at masonry outlets. Firebricks have a very low moisture content, which makes them less likely to crack when exposed to high heat. You'll notice that placing fire bricks in a circle pattern leaves a small, triangle gap between each brick. Be sure to apply mortar along all

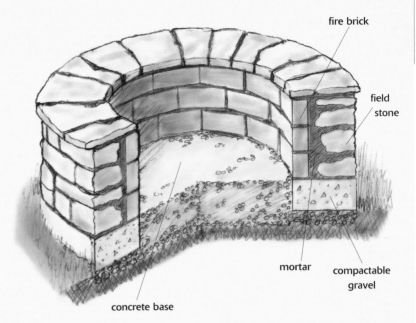

Figure 1

sides of firebricks and use a heavy hand in this crevice to fill the space between the firebricks, and also between the wall. You can use rock debris or mortar to fill space between the firebrick wall and stone wall.

A note on mortar: Carefully butter the bottoms of face stones with mortar, and do not spread mortar flush to the edge of the face stone. Otherwise, when you stack the stones, you'll get an overstuffed sandwich effect. Excess mortar will ooze onto the face of the stone and stain the surface. For a polished look when filling gaps in surface stone, use a jointing tool to smooth mortar between crevices.

Preliminaries

Because you need quite a few supplies for this project, set up a work area by organizing stone into piles, and arranging materials so they are accessible. Make a pile of face stones, capstones, and fire brick. Dedicate an area for mixing mortar; you'll use a wheelbarrow and hoe with holes in it for this task. And consider laying out a tarp to place tools such as trowels and levels. That way, you can keep the yard relatively clean while your masonry work is in progress.

This project features a 5-foot (1.5-m) -diameter pit, with walls that are 18 inches (45.7 cm) high and 12 inches (30.5 cm) wide **(Figure 1)**.

Supplies

- **Fieldstone (1 pallet)**
- **Fire bricks (60 or more depending on dimensions)**
- **Compactable gravel (1 yard)**
- **80-pound bags of premixed gravel mix concrete (4)**
- **18-pound bags of premixed mortar mix (10 to 12)**
- **Shovel**
- **Mixing hoe with holes**
- **Iron rake**
- **Level**
- **Trowels**
- **½-inch (1.3-cm) jointer**
- **Chipping hammer**
- **Stone hammer**
- **Wheelbarrow**
- **Landscape fabric**
- **¼" (6 mm) rebar (20 feet [6 m])**
- **Spray paint (bright orange or yellow)**
- **String**
- **Tape measure**
- **Safety glasses**
- **Chalk**

Steps

1. Select a site. Draw the circle for the pit using a string compass. Loop a piece of string around a pipe or rebar driven into the center of the site. Mark the string at 2½ feet (76 cm). Hold the spray can at this mark, pull the string taut, and walk around the circle painting as you go. This marks the outside of the fire pit. Mark the string at 1½ feet (46 cm) and repeat the painting process. This marks the inside of the fire pit. Between the two lines is the ring where you will lay the footing of the wall.

2. Excavate the area for the footing by digging out 8 inches (20.3 cm) of soil from within the lines **(Figure 2)**. Do not dig out the center circle of grass or dirt at this time. Fill the circle with 2 inches (5 cm) of compactable gravel and tamp down.

3. Mix the concrete in the wheelbarrow, using the hoe. Follow instructions on the package. Spread concrete in the outer circle with a shovel so it forms a ring. Use the iron rake to spread the concrete and eliminate air pockets. When you have 2 inches (5 cm) of concrete in the ring, cut the rebar into 2 foot (61 cm) lengths. Press the rebar, side by side, all around the concrete circle. Add the remaining concrete until even with the surrounding soil. Smooth concrete with a trowel.

4. Allow the concrete to set according to package directions. When set, dig out the remaining inner ring of grass and dirt and fill with compactable gravel. This will allow rain water to drain out of your fire pit.

5. Dry fit the first layer of firebricks around the inner circumference of the footing, with ⅜ inch (1 cm) spacing for mortar joints. On opposite sides of the ring, use pieces of 1 (2 cm) lumber to create a gap that crosses the brick and stone layers. This gap will allow air flow into the fire pit. Place the first layer of face stone around the outer circumference of the footing with ⅜ inch to ½ inch (1 to 1.5 cm) spacing. Use chalk to mark the placements of brick and stone.

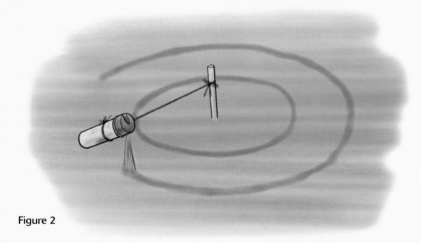

Figure 2

Always check local fire codes
before building your fire pit.

Figure 3

Figure 4

6. Mix the mortar according to package in-structions. Mix small batches at a time. Spread a ½ inch (1.3 cm) layer of mortar on the foot-ing with a trowel. Set your first ring of face stones and fire bricks. Build around the 1 (2 cm) air spacer.

7. Fill the gap between the bricks and stones with junk stone and mortar. Butter the bricks and stones with mortar and lay the second course, alternating the joints so they are not stacked. Smooth joints with jointer. Use a level after completing the second course, to make sure your construction is level **(Figure 3)**. Fill the gap between the two walls. Remove the sticks for the air gap.

8. Continue building the wall. Once the wall is 18 inches (45.7 cm) tall, or the desired height, dry fit capstones across the width of the wall.

9. Set the capstones in a mortar bed. Fill the gaps between capstones with mortar. Smooth with a trowel or jointing tool. Use a level to check that the capstones are level **(Figure 4)**.

10. Create a flame-retardant surrounding for the fire pit. Again, measure and mark a circle around the fire pit by tying a 6½-foot (2-m) -long string to the rebar, and painting an out-line. This measurement accounts for the 2½ foot (0.8-m) radius of the fire pit, and a 4-foot (1.2 m) seating area.

11. Dig out 2 to 3 inches (5.1 to 7.6 cm) of turf and soil, forming a ring around the fire pit. Cut landscape mesh to fit the area, and lay it down, overlapping seams. Spread crushed stone on top of the landscape fabric

PROJECT PAIRINGS

WHILE THE HEAT IS ON, consider these complementary projects:

Make Your Own Stepping Stones 126
Add personal flair to a fire pit area by embedding homemade pavers into your stone seating area.

Interlock Retaining Wall 150
With a base of skills on building stone walls, move on to this advanced project.

PROJECT

Design an Outdoor Kitchen

Don't expect to find picnic fare in outdoor kitchens. Today's backyard chefs can enjoy conveniences like warming drawers and bar sinks—luxury features generally reserved for home kitchens. Grills are equipped with side burners, and refrigeration units include wine storage. These and other appliances available for cooking al fresco rival their indoor counterparts.

You can spend as much or little as you want designing the outdoor kitchen of your dreams. Start with a grill as your centerpiece, and we'll show you how to work from there.

The Dirt

First, set a budget, or the project will easily match the price tag of renovating your home kitchen. A deciding factor in your investment will be how often you expect to use the space. If weather limits your outdoor cooking five months out of the year, you may scale back your grill purchase, or take on the project in phases, adding one feature from your wish list each year. However, year-round grill enthusiasts (like those who flip burgers in the snow) would probably rather cut back the amenities in the home kitchen.

Here are some questions to consider during the planning phase:

- **What kind** of cooking would you like to do outdoors, and how often?
- **Do you eat outside**, or do you grill food and serve it indoors?

Don't allow grill exhaust to smoke out the ambiance of your outdoor party. Grills need to breathe. Equip an enclosed cooking space with a ventilation hood.

- **How close** is your cooking space to an entrance to your home?
- **How many** people cook outdoors at one time?
- **Do mainly** entertain family, or do you host large backyard parties?
- **How many** guests do you usually entertain?
- **Do you rely** on a cooler to chill food and drinks?
- **What existing** landscape features are near the cooking space?
- **Is your grill** on a patio, deck, concrete, or other surface?

Preliminaries

Before you begin, be sure your backyard cooking area is equipped to power your appliances. A refrigerator isn't convenient if you trip over a cord that snakes through plants, over your deck, and into the house. It's a good idea to call an electrician and plumber to evaluate your utility resources before you break ground. You'll need plumbing and drainage, a gas line for your grill, outdoor electrical outlets, and a weather-ready, strong surface as a platform for your grill and food preparation space. In this project, we'll review the basic elements to include in your outdoor kitchen. Personalize the space with projects found in this book, from container gardens to pergola covers.

Steps

1. Get the grill. Your outdoor kitchen will revolve around the grill. You can purchase portable, modular, or custom-design units; or, you may hire a professional to construct a stucco or wood structure to house burners and other components. For starters, try a modular unit. You can begin with the basics: a grill-top and stainless steel cabinet below it. Gradually add side burners, a rotisserie, a refrigerator, a sink, and other conveniences.

2. Establish a surface. Patios are ideal foundations for grills, as the hardscape material can withstand high heat, sparks, and the weight of the equipment itself. If you're starting from scratch, explore the interesting paver products available. (See Brick Paver Patio on page 154.) This "floor" space will set the boundaries for your outdoor kitchen. If your surface is a deck, it may require additional support, depending on the grill and extras like countertops, refrigerators, or cabinets. You'll also want to lay down a fireproof carpet under the grill to protect the deck from grease spills.

3. Prep space. If you cut, marinate, and plate up food indoors, then working in counter space is less of a concern. But the convenience of preparing a meal from start to finish outdoors saves trips back and forth to the home kitchen. Modular grills include options for side work areas.

4. Cool options. Refrigeration will keep food cool until the grill is hot and ready.

5. Lighting. Deck lights, uplighting, path lights, and other low-voltage fixtures will extend cooking hours and add ambiance to the space. (See Install Landscape Lighting on page 184.)

PROJECT PAIRINGS

PREPARE YOUR DECK for cooking with these projects:

PROJECT

Dining al Fresco

For many of us, the deck is an escape—a place to gather with family and friends, a destination for a minivacation right in the back yard. So it makes sense to embellish this al fresco living space, to transform it into something meatier than an informal setup of stackable chairs.

Don't ground your throw rugs, cushy pillows, and elegant lamps from outdoor play. Look inside for design inspiration, and convert a deck into a dining room. These techniques will guide your exterior decoration venture.

The Dirt

You can find affordable outdoor accents that make a big impact at discount stores, including whimsical party lights or inexpensive cloth placemats and decorative pillows. But chances are, you won't have to purchase furniture or invest in tableware to make your deck feel more like home. For just an evening, borrow a lamp from the living room. Or, find use for a throw rug kept in storage by unrolling it on the deck. Your options expand if your deck or patio is under cover, where fabrics, accessories, and furniture are better protected.

In this project, we think beyond traditional patio furniture and accessories. Try choosing one element from each of these categories to set the mood in your outdoor dining room.

Structure

Add walls and a ceiling to your outdoor space by creating a pergola, arbor, or trellises. Closing in your patio or deck gives it a homey feel. Also, these structures provide a framework for hanging lights, fabrics, and pictures.

TEXTURE, COLOR, and a delectable outdoor meal add to the ambiance of your creative table setting.

Furniture

Your table is the patio hub, the centerpiece. Stone surfaces, tumbled marble, and mosaic tabletops look more permanent than plastic tables. These materials also stand up to rain and sun, though nothing warms even an outdoor room like wood. Large Tuscan-style tables can be treated for outdoor use, and you'll want to apply sealant to them annually. Pair a wood table with a combination of bench seating and chairs. A candelabra centerpiece will dress up the table for a formal evening, and fun placemats lighten the mood for picnics.

Lighting

If one element sets the mood, it's lighting. Lace the deck with votive candles or accent pathways with luminaries. Torch lights add spunk to an evening barbecue, and they are not permanent like in-ground landscape lighting fixtures. If your patio has a pergola, you can hang sophisticated chandeliers and candelabras from the rungs. Ransack your holiday decorations and recover the twinkle lights. These dress up trees no matter the season.

Texture

Outdoor fabrics are solution-dyed, so they won't fade from sunlight or mildew. Today you can find these coverings (chair cushion, umbrellas, decorative pillows) in an array of colors and patterns. Look for fabric swatches at specialty stores that carry pool equipment and high-end patio furniture. However, for a one-night stand, living room pillows double as comfortable chair backs. Don't worry about matching colors. Go for a garden variety, which adds interest and looks comfortable rather than stuffy.

Ground cover

The ground cover we're referring to in this project doesn't require water or healthy soil. We're talking rugs, woven floor throws, and basic mats. If your patio is under cover, you'll worry less about the fiber. Go ahead and graduate the old dining room rug to the deck. However, if fading and moisture is a concern, choose natural sisal and jute woven floor coverings. Some polypropylene products mimic this look; they don't stain and can be hosed clean.

Tablescape

Paper tablecloths, napkins, and plates are trusty outdoor standbys, and for good reason. You can use them and lose them. Instead, surprise guests by breaking out a set of dishes retired from regular indoor use. Scout garage sales, flea markets, and consignment shops for vintage china. Again, mix and match for a nostalgic, eclectic effect. Bring salt and pepper shakers outdoors, use flatware rather than plastic forks, and spruce up colorful paper napkins with artistic napkin rings. Finally, finish the table with fresh-cut flowers.

Preliminaries

This project is your roadmap. Refer to the projects listed below to find instructions for making your al fresco dining an ongoing pleasure.

- **Lath Trellis,** page 130
- **Build an Arbor,** page 134
- **Perfect Pergola,** page 138
- **All about Awnings,** page 160
- **Install Landscape Lighting,** page 184
- **Design an Outdoor Kitchen,** page 202

PROJECT PAIRINGS

BESIDES THE SUGGESTED PROJECTS mentioned throughout this chapter, you can add color and texture to your outdoor dining room with plantings. Try these:

Attract Butterflies   90
Attract winged beauties and enjoy the show from your outdoor kitchen.

Herb Garden   94
Harvest flavor from your own backyard.

Cool, Creative Planters   110
Funky or refined? Choose garden containers that suit your personality.

PROJECT

Maximize a Small Space

When green space is no larger than a bungalow half-bath, you learn to make the most of what you've got. Urban dwellers are accustomed to working within the confines of courtyards or rooftop gardens. If you live in a condo, you value the possibilities a container offers as a miniature planting space, and window boxes become your very own backyard (likely within reach of your kitchen sink).

But don't be fooled. A pint-sized space involves the same design principles as a property the size of a township. Make the most of your yard, no matter its shape or size. Techniques and project suggestions in this chapter will help you create a workable blueprint.

The Dirt

As with any landscape project, the first step is to analyze your site. This includes noting the following points: access, shape, and surroundings. This conceptual evaluation should follow careful examination of your property's sun exposure, grade (note slopes or areas with poor drainage), and soil quality. Refer to the checklist in Chapter 1 that addresses lifestyle, design, and property specifics.

Access

Small spaces may be gated, or you may only access the yard by walking through the house and exiting the back door as is typical in some townhouse developments. At best, a narrow walkway may be the only access to your work space. This obviously presents challenges when carting in plant material, hardscape, or other supplies you need to build ponds, patios, pergolas, and such. Make access a critical part of your design. Before you decide *what* to put in your back yard, figure out *how* you will get it there. This may require dividing loads into smaller portions.

Shape

Standard ½- and ¼-acre lots in subdivisions are often squared off, forming a patchwork quilt of box-shaped properties. Small yards are different: skinny, pie-shaped, circular, oblong. This requires planning. Perhaps you utilize every piece of a pie-shaped yard by hardscaping most of it and creating a succulent garden at the tip. An oblong property will look wider if you contrast it with circular patterns, whether a patio, pond, or rounded plantings. Use the principle of contrast to trick the eye.

Purpose

Decide how you prefer to spend time outdoors, and dedicate your small space to this activity—herb gardening, relaxing by a pond, meditating in a Zen space. Once you choose a theme for your small yard, concentrate on how plant material, hardscape, and furniture work together.

Preliminaries

Before you begin, get your plan on paper. Chapter 1 provides instructions on creating a site map, measuring your property, and developing a landscape plan in phases. The process for a small property is no different. Do this first. As you consider features you want to incorporate in the space, refer to the steps in this project for planting and design techniques.

Steps

1. Pick large pots. A collection of small potted plants looks messy and accentuates the fact that you may not actually have room for all of these containers. Instead, combine plantings into large, attractive pots. Remember the odd rule that suggests ones, threes, and so on. are more interesting. Plant in one large pot, or three pots of staggered sizes.

2. Big is better. In large yards, breaking up space into smaller rooms creates intimacy. In small properties, the opposite is true. Dividing an already small area into several tiny spots is a recipe for claustrophobia. Instead, choose one large feature as a focal point, and build interest around this hub. For example, a kidney bean-shaped pond contrasts a linear backyard, and a surrounding patio builds in more room for entertainment. Bordered with layered foliage, greenery blurs the property line and suggests that the space is more expansive.

3. Grow up. Draw the eye up with climbing plants, slender conifers, tall hedges, and hanging baskets. Think of walls, trellis, fencing, and any property border as open ground for planting. Beds of low plantings in a tight space draw the eye down and take up valuable space that may be used for a patio, pond, or other feature.

4. Keep it clean. By choosing plant material that establishes quickly and grows into a jungle of foliage, you'll spend your spare time pruning. A tame, trim look is ideal for small spaces. Opt for slow growers that fill in a bed over time. Train climbing plants to crawl around forms or up lattice and walls. Topiary adds vertical, shapely interest and looks refined. (See Ivy Topiary on page 112.) Maintain shrubbery regularly. (See Tree & Shrub Pruning Clinic on page 36).

5. Blend foliage. Check out your surroundings; look beyond your small lot. Let's say you notice pine trees and mulched areas, or maybe there are flowering shrubs in the distance. By planting similar trees on the border of your lot, you will blur the line between what is yours and what is not. Trickery? Perhaps. But maximizing a small space does require a bit of optical illusion.

COLLECTIONS OF LARGE POTS maximize space efficiently and attractively. Odd numbers of pots make a more effective arrangement.

PROJECT PAIRINGS

TEST THESE PROJECTS in your small space:

Vines for Landscapes   86
Earn more space by including walls, trellis, and fencing as grounds for planting climbers like vines.

Container Planting Clinic   104
Even large potted plants fit well in small spaces.

Create a Pond   178
Choose a high-impact focal point like a pond, and center landscaping around this feature.

Just for Kids!

Creating an outdoor play area for children provides a place for them to imagine, create, and burn off boundless kid energy. The space doesn't need to look like Disney World, and in pursuit of an outdoor living room, you may want to avoid garish jungle gyms. (My parents always found a way to paint the exciting red swing set a bark-colored brown.) Here, we'll show you how to create an attractive sandbox with a cover that creates a children's play zone that blends with your environment.

The Dirt

Imagination is the theme of this Just for Kids backyard plan. We'll convert adult features, such as stepping stones and planters, into kid-friendly delights. Adapt this layout to your outdoor space, and your child's personality.

Your play zone plan may include:
- **Sandbox**
- **Kids' containers** (See Cool, Creative Containers, page 110.)
- **Homemade stepping stones** (See Make Your Own Stepping Stones, page 126.)

Preliminaries

This sandbox project is a step up from the basic board-frame designs. Timber construction makes for a durable play space, and a storage box at one end hides toys. Built-in seats finish the look.

Decide where you will place the sandbox. Prepare this area by marking off a 48 x 96 inch (121.9 x 243.8 cm) area with stakes and string. Remove the turf within the stringed-off area, and dig a flat trench around the perimeter of the sandbox that is 2 inches (5.1 cm) deep by 4 inches (10.2 cm) wide.

Now, you are ready to cut timber pieces and assemble the sandbox.

CREATE A SETTING that encourages children to enjoy the outdoors.

Cutting List

DIAGRAM	PART	LUMBER	SIZE (INCHES/CM)	PCS.
A	Sandbox Sides	4 x 4	92½" (235 cm)	8
B	Sandbox Ends	4 x 4	44½" (113 cm)	8
C	Storage Box Wall	4 x 4	41" (104.1 cm)	4
D	Floorboards	1 x 6	43" (109.2 cm)	3
E	Lid Boards	1 x 8	43½" (110.5 cm)	3
F	Floor & Lid Cleats	2 x 2	18" (45.7 cm)	5
G	Corner Bench Boards	1 x 6	18" w/ 45° angle (45.7 cm)	2
H	Corner Bench Boards	1 x 6	7" w/ 45° angle (17.8 cm)	2
I	Corner Bench Cleats	2 x 2	10" (25.4 cm)	4

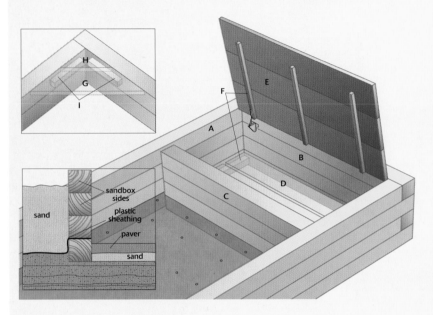

Supplies

- **Shovel**
- **Reciprocating saw**
- **Level**
- **Drill with ³⁄₁₆" (5 mm) bit**
- **Circular saw**
- **Hammer**
- **Utility knife**
- **Miter saw**
- **Coarse gravel**
- **Sand**
- **8-foot 4 x 4 timbers (243.8 x 8.9 x 8.9 cm) (14)**
- **6-foot 1 x 8 lumber (182.9 x 1.9 x 19.1 cm) (2)**
- **8-foot 1 x 6 lumber (243.8 x 1.9 x 14 cm) (2)**
- **6-foot 2 x 2 lumber (182.9 x 1.9 x 1.9 cm) (2)**
- **Wood sealer/protectant**
- **Paintbrush**
- **Heavy duty plastic sheathing**
- **2" (51 mm) galvanized screws**
- **6" (152 mm) barn nails**
- **Pavers**

Steps

1. Use a reciprocating saw to cut all 4 x 4 timbers according to cutting list. Use a circular saw for the rest of lumber (1 x 6s and 2 x 2s).

2. Coat timber and lumber with a wood sealer protectant, allowing it to dry before continuing.

3. Place first tier of sides and ends in the trench. Stagger the corner overlaps so that a long side overlaps one end, but is overlapped by the other end. Level all four corners and add or remove soil as necessary. Drill two pilot holes through timbers at corners, then drive barn nails through pilot holes.

4. Measuring from the inside edge of one end, mark at 18" (45.7 cm) on both sides. Align storage box timber with marks, and then score soil on either side of it (forming a line in the dirt). Remove the timber, and then dig a ¾" (1.9 cm) trench between score marks where the timber will rest.

5. Replace timber into the trench. The top edge will be ¾" (1.9 cm) lower than the edge of the first tier of the sandbox wall. Add or remove dirt until timber is level. Drill pilot holes through sandbox sides into the ends of storage box timber. Drive barn nails through pilot holes.

6. Pour a 2-inch (5.1-cm) -deep bed of gravel into the sandbox (not storage area). Rake gravel smooth. Cover gravel bed with heavy duty plastic sheathing. Pierce plastic with a screwdriver every foot (0.3 m) to form drainage holes **(Figure 1)**.

7. Set the second tier of timbers in place over the first tier over plastic sheathing, staggering the joints over the first tier. Drill pilot holes every 24" (60.9 cm) along the lengths of the timbers, then drive barn nails through pilot holes.

8. Repeat step 7 for remaining tiers, staggering the joints and nails.

9. Finish the storage box by stacking remaining storage box timbers over the first one. Drill

ASSEMBLY NOTE

- All pilot holes are ³⁄₁₆ inch (4.8 mm).

- Barn nails are all 6 inches (15.2 cm).

- Follow these requirements unless steps indicate otherwise.

pilot holes through the sandbox sides into the ends of the timbers. Drive barn nails into pilot holes **(Figure 2)**. Cut excess plastic from outside of sandbox timbers.

10. Position a floor cleat against each side wall along the bottom of the storage box, attaching them with 2" (51 mm) galvanized nails.

11. Place floorboards over cleats. Leave a ½" (1.3 cm) gap between each board to allow drainage. Use 2" (51 mm) screws to fasten floor boards to cleats.

12. Assemble the lid. Place lid pieces side by side, ends flush. Lay three cleats across the lid, one at each end and one in the middle. Drill pilot holes and attach cleats with 2" (51 mm) galvanized screws.

13. Attach the lid to the sandbox frame with hinges and included hardware. Prevent lid from opening past a 90 degree angle by installing a toy box lid support on the underside of the sandbox frame. (You can purchase an approved support from a hardware store.)

Figure 2

Figure 3

14. Finally, build corner benches. Mark ¾" (1.9 cm) from the top edge of the sandbox at each corner. Align the top edge of bench cleats with the mark, and fasten them at the corners with 2" (51 mm) galvanized screws.

15. Wedge smaller bench piece into the corner, resting it on the cleats. Attach it with 2" (51 mm) screws. The larger bench piece fits next to this one. Attach it to cleats with screws. Repeat this step for second corner bench **(Figure 3)**.

16. Now, you're ready to fill the sandbox to a depth of 7" (17.8 cm). Install a paver border around your sandbox to finish the look, if desired.

Figure 1

PROJECT PAIRINGS

THESE PROJECTS will appeal to children:

Attract Butterflies   90
Teach children about nature's painted ladies by creating a habitat for butterflies.

Container Planting Clinic   104
Teach children the basics of gardening in a pint-sized environment.

Build a Birdhouse   146
Everyone can help construct this project, and your children will enjoy watching winged wonders visit your yard.

Seasonal Maintenance Tips

No matter the season, there are plenty of ways to continue your outdoor pursuits. When temperatures drop, take handiwork like making a hypertufa planter, (page 98) or building a birdhouse, (page 146) indoors. Concerning lawn care activities, such as mowing or mulching, you can prepare for summer by doing mechanical tune-ups during winter.

Of course, your lawn care responsibilities will vary depending on whether you live in a cool or warm climate. Refer to one of the following checklists that correspond with your weather, and exercise that green thumb year-round.

Cool Climates

SPRING

- **Service lawn mower:** sharpen blades, change oil and filter, general tune-up (if you did not do so during winter, the ideal time).
- **Plant annuals** appropriate to the climate.
- **Clean up leaves** and other debris cluttering beds.
- **Lay fresh mulch** in landscape beds to discourage weed growth and help plant roots retain moisture.
- **Seed bare spots** in your lawn, or over-seed (if you did not perform these tasks in fall).
- **Prevent weeds** by applying a preemergent application, but consult a lawn care professional first.
- **Spot-treat weeds** as needed.
- **Apply slow-acting fertilizer** to promote green-up.

SUMMER

- **Adjust mower** to the proper height for your turf variety; raise height to alleviate summer stress in cool-season grasses.
- **Water** lawn as needed.

FALL

- **Cut back** plant branches after the first hard freeze.
- **Dead-head** perennial flowers by pinching off expired blooms; this encourages new growth in spring.
- **Aerate** your lawn in early fall, if necessary.
- **Seed bare patches** or new lawns in early fall to allow time for germination and root development before winter.
- **Remove leaves** from your yard and plant beds.
- **Apply** a fall fertilizer application.

USDA Miscellaneous Publication No. 1475. Issued January 1990. Authored by Henry M. Cathey while Director, U.S. National Arboretum For additional information, see the website at www.usna.usda.gov/Hardzone/ushzmap.html.

Warm Climates

The same equipment maintenance reminders apply in warm climates. But because warm-season grasses love hot, southern weather, spring and summer are the best times to plant.

SPRING AND SUMMER

- **Plant new lawns** or repair dead spots in your yard.
- **Fertilize** and follow a regular lawn care program with pesticide applications as needed. (Note: A professional will best advise you on these preventive and curative applications.)
- **Water** lawn as needed.
- **Adjust mower height** to appropriate level based on your turfgrass variety; cut lawn when needed.
- **Aerate** or dethatch, if necessary.
- **Plant annuals.**

FALL AND WINTER

- **Service** lawn equipment.
- **Lay fresh** mulch in beds.
- **Water** growing lawns on a regular basis.

WINTER

- **Take your mower** in for service before the spring rush (sharpen blades, general tune-up).
- **Conduct an inventory** of your tools. What are you missing? What needs to be replaced? Which tools need sharpening or cleaning?
- **Trim back trees and shrubs.** (Note: You can trim moderately year-round.)

USDA Plant Hardiness Zone Map

USDA Plant Hardiness Zone Map

ZONE	
1	Below -50F (Below -45.6C)
2a	-50 to -45F (-42.8 to -45.5C)
2b	-45 to -40F (-40.0 to -42.7C)
3a	-40 to -35F (-37.3 to -39.9C)
3b	-35 to -30F (-34.5 to -37.2C)
4a	-30 to -25F (-31.7 to -34.4C)
4b	-25 to 20F (-28.9 to -31.6C)
5a	-20 to -15F (-26.2 to -28.8C)
5b	-15 to -10F (-23.4 to -26.1C)
6a	-10 to -5F (-20.6 to -23.3C)
6b	-5 to 0F (-17.8 to -20.5C)
7a	0 to 5F (-15.0 to 17.7C)
7b	5 to 10F (-12.3 to -14.9C)
8a	10 to 15F (-9.5 to -12.2C)
8b	15 to 20F (-6.7 to -9.4C)
9a	20 to 25F (-3.9 to -6.6C)
9b	25 to 30F (-1.2 to -3.8C)
10a	30 to 35F (1.6 to -1.1C)
10b	35 to 40F (4.4 to 1.7C)
11	above 40F (above 4.5C)

Resources

All About Lawns
www.allaboutlawns.com

American Lawns
www.american-lawns.com

The American Ivy Society, Inc.
PO Box 2123, Naples, FL 34106-2123
www.ivy.org

Aquascape Designs
www.aquascapedesigns.com

Ask the Builder
Tim Carter
www.askthebuilder.com

Avalon Artistic Landscape Lighting
www.avalonlighting.com

Barnes Nursery
Huron, Ohio
Sue Cross
www.barnesnursery.com

The Betty Mills Company
www.bettymills.com

Colorado State Cooperative Extension
www.ext.colostate.edu

Compost Guide
www.compostguide.com

Finley Products, Inc.
www.2x4basics.com

Georgia-Pacific
www.gp.com

How to Compost.org
www.howtocompost.org

Hunter Industries
www.hunterindustries.com

ICI Paints (Glidden)
www.icipaints.com

John Deere
www.johndeere.com
Customer Contact Center: (800) 537-8233

Know Before You Mow
www.knowbeforeyoumow.org

Lowe's Home Improvement
www.lowes.com

Mississippi State University
Research and Extension System
www.msucares.com

North Carolina State University
North Carolina State Cooperative Extension
www.ces.ncsu.edu/index.php?page=lawngarden

O'Neill Landscape Design and Installation
Chagrin Falls, Ohio
Heidi O'Neill
www.heidioneill.com

Penn State Center for Turfgrass Science
http://turf.cas.psu.edu/

Purdue University
Cooperative Extension Service
www.agcom.purdue.edu

Randall Whitehead Lighting Solutions
Randall Whitehead
www.randallwhitehead.com

Thomas Sanderson Ltd.
www.thomas-sanderson.co.uk

The Home Depot
www.homedepot.com

The Irrigation Association
www.irrigation.org
(703) 536-7080

The Ohio State University Extension
http://extension.osu.edu/index.php
(614) 292-6181

The Plant Press
Dictionary of Common Names
www.plantpress.com/dictionary

Summerwood Outdoors, Inc.
www.summerwood.com

University of Arizona
College of Agriculture and Life Sciences
http://ag.arizona.edu/

University of Kentucky
Entomology
www.uky.edu/Ag/Entomology/

University of Minnesota
Extension
www.extension.umn.edu

Viking
www.vikingrange.com

Index

Photographer Credits

Alamy/JG Photography/www.alamy.com, 204

Courtesy of Avalon Artistic Landscape Lighitngwwwavalonlighting.com, 185

Courtesy of Hunter Industries, 5

Courtesy of ICI Paints/www.icipaints.com, 146; 172; 173

Courtesy of John Deere/www.johndeere.com, 25; 31 (bottom); 34; 39; 58

Dency Kane/www.dencykane.com, 13; 60; 66; 81; 106; 111 (bottom, left & right); 126; 144; 151; 165

Dency Kane/www.dencykane.com/Mary Forsberg, Designer, 155

Dency Kane/www.dencykane.com/Brian Kissinger, Designer, 182

Dency Kane/www.dencykane.com/Kyoko Nagai Kitadai, Designer, 119

Dency Kane/www.dencykane.com/Carol Mercer & Lisa Verderosa, Secret Garden, Ltd., 73

Dency Kane/www.dencykane.com/Peconoic River Herb Farm, 95

Dency Kane/www.dencykane.com/Mike Platta, Designer, 198

Dency Kane/www.dencykane.com/Dean Riddle, Designer, 108

Clive Nichols/www.clivenichols.co.uk, 7; 11; 91; 105; 111 (top, right); 158; 178; 191; 207; 211

Allan Penn, 27; 49; 54; 128; 186; 187

Courtesy of Thomas Sanderson Ltd./www.thomas-sanderson.co.uk, 161; 162

Courtesy of Viking/www.vikingrange.com, 202

Jessie Walker/www.jessiewalker.com, 3; 4; 9; 33; 37; 43; 53; 57; 69; 76; 84; 87; 102; 111 (top, left); 112; 115; 123; 124; 131; 135; 138; 141; 168; 170; 177; 195

Acknowledgments

A book designed to keep you, dear reader, busy every weekend of the year requires reinforcements on the creative end to be sure that all measurements, each description, and every detailed illustration and glossy, inspiring photo make your job easier. This beautiful package is the product of a talented group.

Cheers to "Team 52!"

In particular, Karen Ruth, whose deep expertise in all things technical is imprinted in every project. She figured and reconfigured the measurements, raked through the logistics, and mentally tested each step to be sure our fearless (and very busy) readers would not stumble over any process. She's a whiz! And I'm grateful for her well-trained copyeditor's eye. Thanks to Karen for asking the tough questions, and for patience and commitment to this project.

To Betsy, our ringleader and guide—the glue. Detective Betsy unearthed amazing photography for this book. Counselor Betsy assured a frazzled (and borderline insane, at times) writer that yes, she is normal. (A little white lie never hurt anyone.) General Betsy kept us on track, on time, and on our toes. She ushered an intimidating manuscript (doesn't 52 projects wear you out just thinking of it?!) through a thoughtful process to produce what you see here. This book was gratifying and enjoyable to write because she was there every step of the way, with support and answers and warm-fuzzies in the form of "you-go-girl" e-mails. Those are so important.

To our industrious illustrator, Chuck Lockhart, for giving readers the visuals to understand each project and the nuts-and-bolts imagery to guide them through complicated steps. These beautiful renderings, so carefully crafted, help tell the story—they are the story in many cases. Thank you.

To David Martinell, Rosalind Wanke and Cora Hawks at Quayside Publishing and designer John Hall, for producing another visually stunning book that carries their expertise and creative stamp.

My most sincere appreciation to the John Deere team. You'll keep everyone busy with this book! Thank you Bill Klutho, Dean Hamke, Greg Weekes, Jennifer Cox, Mike Ballou, and Stephanie Boozer. It has truly been my pleasure to write this project and its predecessor, John Deere's Lawn Care & Landscaping. Thank you for entrusting me with creative license and for providing invaluable resources that have made this and other projects possible. This opportunity is a gift.

Haven, this is to our test site in Bay Village, Ohio. We've got a lot of work to do! And I have a feeling that Grandpa Gates will be watching to make sure those roses are just right.

About the Author

Kristen Hampshire is an award-winning writer whose work has been published in a range of national magazines. A curious mind draws Hampshire into diverse topics, from corporate profiles to women's health, travel, and the arts. Her specialty is in style, design, and how these elements merge outdoors in the landscape. She covers these subjects regularly for consumer publications. She is the author of three books, including *John Deere's Lawn Care & Landscaping*, © 2007 by Quarry Books, and served as an editor for a green-industry publication for the landscape industry. Hampshire and her business, WriteHand Co., are based at home in Bay Village, Ohio.

Learn more about John Deere's Lawn Care series and Hampshire's writing on www.kristenhampshire.com.

Notes